POWER
OF THE
INNER
SELF

Also by Maureen Garth:

Starbright

Moonbeam

Sunshine

The Inner Garden

InnerSpace

THE POWER OF THE INNER SELF

A Book of Healing

MAUREEN GARTH

HarperCollins*Publishers*

To my darling Eleanor
Who fills me with love and inspiration

HarperCollins*Publishers*

First published in Australia in 1996
by HarperCollins*Publishers* Pty Limited
ACN 009 913 517
A member of the HarperCollins*Publishers* (Australia) Pty Limited Group

Copyright © 1996 Maureen Garth

This book is copyright.
Apart from any fair dealing for the purposes of private study, research, criticism or review, as permitted under the Copyright Act, no part may be reproduced by any process without written permission.
Inquiries should be addressed to the publishers.

HarperCollins*Publishers*
25 Ryde Road, Pymble, Sydney, NSW 2073, Australia
31 View Road, Glenfield, Auckland 10, New Zealand
77-85 Fulham Palace Road, London W6 8JB, United Kingdom
Hazelton Lanes, 55 Avenue Road, Suite 2900, Toronto, Ontario M5R 3L2
and 1995 Markham Road, Scarborough, Ontario M1B 5M8, Canada
10 East 53rd Street, New York NY 10032, USA

National Library of Australia Cataloguing-in-Publication data:

Garth, Maureen.
  The power of the inner self: a book of healing.
  ISBN 0 7322 5808 1.
  1. Meditation. 2. Meditations. I. Title.
158.12

Edited by Kevin Mark Editorial and Literary Services
Cover: *Float Free*, a painting by Australian artist Lucille Martin © 1988.
Acrylic, photocollage and gold leaf on canvas 91.5 × 66 cm
Cover photography by Graham Munro
Printed in Australia by Griffin Press

9 8 7 6 5 4 3 2 1
99 98 97 96

Part One: *Introducing Meditation*

Meditation and healing 3

What is meditation? 16

Meditation and visualisation 22

Karma 26

The aura 31

The chakras 37

Illness in my life 44

Illness and Ian Gawler 50

Taking control 52

Healing and the power of prayer 54

Healing and grief 58

Healing with colour 68

Absent healing 73

How to give spiritual healing 78

Having an open mind like a child 82

Using the visualisations in this book 85

Meditating in groups 90

Meditating alone 93

Making the visualisations your own 94

Part Two: *The Visualisations*

The star prelude 97

The wise old tree 99

A basket of crystals 102

The value of the self and beliefs 106

Your spiritual waterfall and chakras 110

Contents

The large rock and its many caves   114
The pool, the lights and the dolphins   117
The golden bell   121
Becoming one with everything in the Universe   124
The pyramid   127
Cleansing your chakras with colour   131
The rays of light   134
Conception   138
Your unborn child   142
The stars and the miniature waterfall   145
Your soul, your spirit   148
Healing with colour   151
The river of life and the rainbow   155
World healing   159
Earth cleansing   162
Grief and loss   166
Releasing stress   169
The Summerland   173
The healing sanctuary   177
Healing relationships   180
Healing your inner child   184
The healing chair   188
The moon and your emotions   191
Your skeletal structure   194
Heavenly nectar   198
References and suggested reading   201

PART ONE:

Introducing Meditation

Meditation & Healing

The mind is a powerful instrument. It has an amazing capacity to deal with difficulties that may at first appear to us to be impossible to overcome. It can also show us avenues that can bring resolution to, or an escape route from, particular problems that we encounter at various stages of our lives. The mind has the ability to direct us in life, to show us that the possibilities open to us are endless, and that all things have solutions.

We generally take our mind for granted, without giving deep thought to its marvellous qualities. I believe there is nothing we cannot accomplish, if we use our mind in the right way. If we use it in a positive fashion, then positive things bloom in our life. Our mind deals well with positive thought and input; by maintaining positive thoughts, our lives can be altered so that we experience the best life has to offer.

Because our mind is so powerful, it can even change the course of our illnesses. When we use the power of our mind to heal ourselves, we experience a different dimension of consciousness and a new thought process. By going deeply into the meditative state - where we use visualisation to facilitate healing - we allow our mind and body to work as one, and we accept at a deep inner level that our mind and our body can be healed.

When we meditate, we go into an altered state that allows the healing energies to penetrate deeply within. By using creative visualisation - which most people find easy to use - in our meditation, we can alter our illness and bring peace and serenity into our being.

Because our minds are such amazingly powerful instruments, they retain images and thoughts that have long been forgotten. Some of these images and thoughts may have a negative content that could still be having an effect upon our physical being. If we continue to be absorbed by negative thoughts, then everything we do will be coloured by negativity. If your mind is used in a negative way, then the negative pathway is the pathway you will traverse. You may not only find it difficult to remove the negative thoughts from your mind, but may have difficulty in breaking the negative cycle. If you say 'I can't do that,' 'I'm no good at it' or 'I'm sure I will fail,' then your mind accepts that these things are true for you and actually makes them a reality by making them come to pass.

Unfortunately negativity flourishes well if it is fed, and there are many people who do such a good job of feeding their negativity that they have little time for anything positive in their lives. We hear some people saying things such as 'Oh, I always have bad luck,' 'I never feel well,' 'I'm not good enough for that job,' 'Why try when I know it won't work' or 'It always happens to me'. And then they wonder why they have bad luck, never feel well, do not get the job, or why things do not work out well in their lives! We should be very conscious of the words we use and the way we speak, as our negative talk can cause many things to rebound upon on us in our lives, thus giving them reality.

The latter saying - 'It always happens to me' - seems to be a favourite with many people. I am certain that whatever they are expecting to happen, which is always something negative, will happen to them. By making statements such as this, they are accepting that they have no control over their lives or their situations, which is untrue.

We must take control of our lives, we must take personal responsibility for all our actions and our thoughts. Why allow negative thoughts to control our minds and our lives, when these negative thoughts have such a detrimental impact upon our health? If we allow ourselves to move into self-pity, which, of course, is self-destructive, we will generally find that depression is the result. How much better it is to live with positive rather than negative thoughts, and to have a more fulfilling life as a result.

If people were to put as much energy into positive thoughts as they often put into negative ones, they would find their lives would be rewarding at many levels. Negative thoughts have a life force of their own, and I believe negative thoughts can create ill health. On the other hand, positive thoughts encourage growth and balance in what we do, at all levels of our existence, resulting in a healthy mind and body. Our thought patterns influence our behaviour, which in turn influences our health and wellbeing.

Many people focus upon their dis-ease, instead of their health, and they love to talk about their illness. Their illness seems to have taken a prime place of importance in their lives, instead of their health. If you stop and think about your speech pattern, particularly how you have been expressing yourself to others about your ill health, you may find that you are accepting that this state of ill health belongs with you. Instead of focusing on the negative, you should concentrate on seeing yourself having a healthy mind and body, on being a person who is full of energy and vitality, one who wants to live life to the fullest.

If we believe the mind flowers through the nourishment of strong positive thought, then we know that we can use the power of the mind to overcome difficulties with our health. Each of us has the ability to use our mind to assist in healing the illness within our body, and some of the tools we can use to achieve this are meditation, visualisation, colour, sound, prayer and positive thought.

We need positive thoughts to ensure that we obtain beneficial results from the healing energies that we can work with while in the meditative state. There are many illnesses that could be healed by the self, provided the mind is focused, receptive and uncluttered. We also need to believe that we deserve to be healed. This sounds very simple, yet it works.

By changing your negative thought patterns into positive ones, your health and your life can be vastly improved. Because the images impressed in the subconscious from previous experiences cannot be easily recalled, it is good to instil in your mind positive thoughts about your expected healing. The very act of having negative thoughts regarding your self-healing will mean that you have failed before you have begun.

A positive attitude, accompanied by perseverance and a desire to succeed, can bring results that may surprise you. Feel yourself becoming a tree, your roots entering the earth, a profusion of green leaves growing from your branches, which give shelter to others. Experience the nourishment you are receiving from the earth, the heavenly waters that flow from the billowing clouds above, and the warmth from the glowing golden sun, and you will feel yourself growing as the tree does. Think of yourself as being this beautiful large tree, whose roots are deep and secure, whose inner strength and security flows out to meet all challenges, and who has a profound love for life and living.

When you are not well, work on yourself in the meditative state by bringing healing energies around you and by seeing yourself achieving optimum health. If, however, the illness continues for any length of time, then seek the services of a doctor or a respected healer. But continue to work on yourself by combining meditation with visualisation, so as to improve your health. See your life force becoming brighter as you do so.

Nowadays there are many ways in which we can seek assistance with illness, including medical practitioners, osteopaths, naturopaths, homoeopathy, herbalists, Feldenkris method, chiropractors, Bowen technique, spiritual healing, mental healing, Alexander technique, acupuncture, rebirthing, Gestalt therapy, hypnotherapy, bach flowers, bush flowers, Kinesiology, psychotherapy, Reiki, macrobiotics, polarity therapy, craniosacral work, massage, Chinese herbs - and many more. Because there are so many different options available, ask your friends for recommendations, either people they have seen themselves or who have been recommended to them.

There are many different types of illness:

- physical
- mental
- emotional
- stress-related
- anxiety-related
- phobias.

It is how we accept and deal with our illness that changes the balance of things. The mind is such a powerful tool that we can use it to project the state of health we desire. We do not have to accept that our illness will stay with us always. The way we think and our inner perceptions can help to change the course of our illness.

We need to not only look at why we have become ill in the first place, but why that illness has a place in our lives. Some people need illness to make them feel protected and secure. While they are ill, others will gather around and support them, and they feel needed and cared for. This may not occur if the illness was not there. Although on one level they want optimum health, on another they fear that the support they are receiving while being ill may be withdrawn if this occurs. This is learned behaviour - it has been their experience that ill health has given them the attention they need that was not forthcoming in their life and relationships. It could be that this learned behaviour started early in life, when getting attention from their parents, favourite aunt or uncle, or friends. It could also be that they grew up in a negative environment and have learned to accept negativity as a necessary part of life.

Yet if their emotional needs were met, and they allowed themselves to move away from fear and negativity and the possibility of rejection, they would feel centred and at peace within. Both their body and mind would respond with vibrant health.

Illness often starts in the mind, and the state of our mind affects our body. It is important to think along lines that are good for us. How we think, how we act, how we deal with situations in our life, can be reflected back into the physical body either by ill health or by the feeling of being on top of the world.

How we think about ourselves determines how well we feel. If we believe we are worthless, not only do we feel worthless but our entire person suffers. At various times life does not always run smoothly, and we are often under stress. If we do not deal well with these difficulties, and if we allow depression or stress to control our lives, the result may be illness.

Everyone experiences stress, and no one appears able to escape from it. Being delayed by transport problems that are out of your control - the bus or train being late, your car breaking down - being unable to live up to someone else's expectations of who you are, or being unable to live up to your own expectations, learning new computer programs, running a home, money problems, working, dealing with difficult people, meeting the mortgage or rent payments, relationships and dealing with peer pressure, can all be very stressful situations. A certain amount of stress is good for us, but sometimes we end up buckling under the pressure and feel we can no longer cope. My visualisation **Releasing stress** (see p.169) enables you to do just that: release the stress from your mind and your body. After entering your peaceful garden, you are taken by a golden lion to an old tree who will absorb the stress within your body, taking it deep within his thick trunk before releasing it into the atmosphere as electrical sparks through his uppermost leaves.

All of my visualisations are tools to assist you in your self-healing, with strong imagery that will spark your own images, according to your individuality.

By letting go of stress or fear, you will be able to create new and more positive experiences in your life. See your life as being a marvellous opportunity for growth and development, and also see your experiences as being constructive. Feel the freedom and release this approach brings to your inner person as the stress leaves your body and your mind. By letting go of any stress or fear that is or has been holding you back, you will then find everything will be reflected back to you in a positive way, including good health and vitality.

Pain is a signal there is something wrong and that there is an imbalance in our energy field that may have recent or longstanding origins. The sensation of pain is produced by our nervous system, which sends signals to our brain. If we believe that illness is caused by an imbalance between the body, mind and spirit, then the restoration of that balance will not only create glowing health, but harmony within.

We need to assume a positive attitude towards our healing. If it is entered into in a half-hearted manner, then the results may also be half-hearted. Often there is a need to work on our mental attitude in order to attain harmony between our mental, emotional and physical attributes.

Some people live in a constant state of chaos that may make it difficult for healing to commence. If your life is always in a state of flux and stress, meditation can help to change that as well as allowing you to heal. When you go deeply into your altered state, ideas and thoughts will surface that may show you how to deal with your problems in a different fashion. This will help you retain a good mental attitude about what you want in your life and will also aid in your healing process.

Meditation can make you more conscious of your surroundings, more aware of people and their needs, more tolerant of the failings of others, and more forgiving of your own failings. Illness may come about because we have lost direction and purpose in our lives. Meditation can give us the strength we need to allow different avenues to open up that will enable us to work on ourselves and to enhance our daily life and living.

By becoming more tolerant of others' failings and more forgiving of your own, your attitude will change. You will become more loving, more hopeful, more honest, and more at peace within. Being at peace frees you from fear, making you willing to change and allowing healing to begin.

We are often harder on ourselves than we are on others. Perhaps we need to look at why we feel so harshly towards ourselves, and allow more love and forgiveness to flow from our heart, our being, into not only our physical selves, but into our spiritual selves as well.

We not only have a physical body, but other bodies that surround it. When we take healing through our physical body, it also enters our luminous bodies, that is, our etheric, mental, emotional and spiritual bodies. The etheric body is a blueprint of the physical, and whatever ills we have are shown there very strongly. Therefore when healing the body the etheric, which stands so closely to the physical, needs also to be healed.

I believe we have a Higher Self, and that through meditation we can make contact with this essence or energy force to find our direction in life, to aid in the healing process and to bring peace and serenity into our life, our soul, our person. I believe our Higher Self has accumulated the experiences of our many lives spent here on earth and that we are, at this time, only an aspect of this higher consciousness. Because our Higher Self has knowledge of the problems encountered over these eons of time, it also has a great ability to help us deal with the problems of the present time.

I also believe we can receive guidance not only from our Higher Self but also from people who exist on a different plane. Some people may refer to them as angels or spirit guides. When you meditate you may sometimes 'see' people in your garden who speak with you and give you spiritual guidance. They may also speak about what is happening in your physical life. The spiritual and physical are linked, and one cannot exist without the other.

Meditation and visualisation can be used as aids to heal the body. When meditating, we can use our visualisation skills to assist in healing the part of the body that is dis-eased or in other need. Going into the meditative state enables our bodies to more fully receive the healing being projected by our mind, so that it deeply enters our subconscious. Our subconscious can then work on the problem we have given it.

Our inner self is extremely powerful and it has the ability to aid the body in its healing. If we unleash the power within ourselves, we can operate at all levels of our life with the optimum in health, vitality and enthusiasm, and with a real zest for life and living.

Not only can we liberate our power and use it to self-heal and maintain our health, but we can also assist others in the healing process. We all possess an innate ability to heal others, as well as ourselves. This is apparent when we comfort someone who is in pain, or upset by a person or a situation that they cannot understand or control. They feel better afterwards because our ministrations have released a healing energy that brings understanding and peace. When a child comes to its mother after a fall, the mother soothes the child, placing her hands on the injured part of the child's body, and the healing commences. The child runs away to play with others, or to return perhaps to the trampoline from which she fell and hurt herself, feeling secure and with the pain having disappeared. My daughter, Eleanor, always comes and asks me for healing whenever she is unwell or upset by events in her life. She accepts that she will be healed - and she is.

We can also send healing to people who are not in our immediate vicinity. We can do this by using the power of our inner self to visualise the person, their illness and healing rays sent to assist them in recovering from their ordeal. If we realised how strong we can be by releasing our inner energies, our inner power, we would be assisting not only ourselves but others in a way that would benefit many.

Not all people are going to be healed from their illness. For instance, the illness may be incurable but, by directing healing rays and positivity into the seat of their illness, we can bring a sense of peace and serenity to the person who is in need, or to ourselves if it is our illness that requires the healing rays. If you do not know why you have attracted your illness, perhaps you need to bless it and to see this illness as an opportunity for growth at a different level. If your illness is incurable, then it is how you handle your illness and the people around you that makes the difference between dying without fear, but with grace and dignity, rather than dying in a fearful state of mind.

Many illnesses are such that they appear hopeless, but healing miracles have been recorded - not only throughout the ages, but also in recent times. Have hope and faith that the healing you are receiving or giving will change the course of the illness, and ask a Higher Power to aid in bringing about optimum health, if this is meant to be.

All healing comes from a Higher Source. This source may be called by different names, such as Mother, Father, God, Goddess, The Absolute, Universal Consciousness,

Higher Power and the God Force. For simplicity, I have used the terms the 'God Force' or 'Higher Power' throughout this book.

I believe that all healing coming from this Higher Power is spiritual healing, and that we can ask this Higher Power to assist us in the healing of ourselves and others.

If we have a strong belief that something such as this Higher Power exists beyond ourselves, then we should believe that it has the power to assist us in healing the self and others. One of the ways we can have contact with this God Force for our healing is through the power of prayer or meditation. By sitting quietly in the meditative state, our bodies are given the opportunity to self-heal.

What is Meditation?

Meditation allows us to enter a space within ourselves where we feel complete, where we can surrender the self, allowing it to feel a depth of love and peace that perhaps has not been available or able to be reached in our physical lives. Meditation enables us to get in touch with the spiritual depths of our being, in a place where there is peace and serenity. If our inner being is serene, imagine how we can project this serenity into our lives and onto other people. Meditation is taking the time to sit quietly in order to gain this peace and serenity.

Many of the things that have worried or irritated us can take on a different perspective with meditation. Our focus changes and we can see our problems in a different light. We find ourselves able to deal with people and situations in a calmer and more centred fashion than before. We feel less stressed and more able to cope with difficulties that may present themselves. And very importantly, we can find ourselves becoming kinder not only to others, but also to ourselves.

Meditation can give us stability. We are made up of physical, mental, emotional and spiritual components, and we should take the time to nourish our body, mind, emotions and the spiritual essence within, our Higher Self. My belief is that our Higher Self has unlimited wisdom and love, and is there to help us if we trust in it and allow it to. During meditation it is possible to communicate with this aspect of oneself, to listen, and to receive guidance and advice.

Life today is very competitive and more stressful than ever before. We are always in a hurry, with little time to spare. We tend to eat food on the run and our bodies can feel out of kilter if we do not take time out for the self. Some people find it difficult to face ageing, while others are troubled by the prospect of being left on their own. Sometimes it can be difficult to express ourselves emotionally. Meditation can help to alleviate our difficulties by changing our thought and feeling processes, allowing us to slow down, become more centred, to experience tranquillity and to feel whole and complete within.

Because of life's frenetic pace, we seldom take time out to feel our inner peace, to experience seclusion. We do not have to sit on a mountain top for the beautiful experiences that meditation can give us, nor to feel the inner glow of serenity, calmness and peace that naturally comes to us from being in this state. By allowing ourselves this gentle but powerful experience, we are opening ourselves up to the Universe and acknowledging there is a Higher Power. If we accept that the Universe and the Higher Power will provide, and that we are connected to these energies, then we will be able to accept that we have the ability to heal ourselves and to help others with their healing.

Meditation means going to a place within where we are in contact with our spiritual essence, the part of the self that is not obvious to others. Meditation allows us to reach depths where we can access the knowledge that may be needed by various levels of ourselves for our wellbeing, and it plays a vital part in our ability to heal our bodies. By meditating, and particularly by focusing on the healing properties of meditation, we bring into play the body's ability to be brought into line with the truly spiritual, mental and emotional aspects of the self, enabling healing to commence.

When we meditate, we gain many benefits. We allow stress to leave our body, our blood pressure drops and both our heart beat and breathing slows. By meditating each day, even for a short period, we feel more relaxed and able to cope with the effects of everyday life.

Meditation has brought a lot of joy and peace into my own life. Just being able to sit quietly and to feel contact with the God Force has enhanced my life.

When we meditate, we go into a place of seclusion, into our inner space, our inner self, in order to heal the body. By going into this meditative state, we are allowing ourselves to experience the peace and serenity that is at the core of our being.

It is important to take time out to nourish our inner person or our needs may suffer, particularly if we are living at a pace that is inappropriate for us. In order to feel strong spiritually and to cope with the difficulties that we encounter in life, we need more peace and quiet within ourselves.

Meditation has been practised throughout the ages and in many different cultures. It is used in churches, Buddhist temples, ashrams, mosques and synagogues, as well as in homes and by communing with nature in the open air. Meditation means going inside the self, allowing peace and serenity to enter, and coming in contact with the Higher Power or your own Higher Self. Meditation allows you to listen to the inner self, to become in tune, not only with the self, but with nature and with all that lives on our plane of existence. Some people like to meditate to a mantra, to a sound, to quiet music or to a prayer. And others require nothing but silence.

Our body is both male and female. The left side of the body is female and the right side male. In the brain this is reversed - the right side is female, the left side male. The male, or left, side of the brain is the logical side, the one that dictates order and symmetry in life. This side of the brain can sometimes be too logical and dominant, and not allow the more intuitive and creative right side much latitude. Meditation brings into use the right, or female, side of the brain and allows it to be creative and intuitive. It enables us to create the pictures or images of ourselves, who we want to be, and how we want our lives to develop.

Creativity flows when we allow our right brain to take control and we become more in touch with our feminine side. The logical left side may demand we have constructive thoughts and not allow our thoughts to drift. What is needed, of course, is for both sides to work well together, each allowing the other its own space. We spend most of our waking hours being logical and in control. When we meditate we allow ourselves to experience a beautiful creative energy that we may otherwise only rarely feel.

If we learn to meditate daily, we should find ourselves becoming more focused and centred, more able to deal with the genuine problems, as well as the trivia, that enters and causes distress in our lives. Some of the benefits to be found can be a sense of peacefulness, of serenity and of vitality, as well as a calmness that may be difficult to achieve otherwise.

Initially you may find it easier to spend several short periods of time in meditation. As you become used to the meditative state and find yourself going deeper and deeper within, you may want to meditate for longer periods of time. You will know what is the right length of time for you. There is no set time. If you feel an hour will bring you more benefits, then by all means spend that time. If you feel more comfortable with two half-hour sessions, or perhaps with ten minutes both morning and night, then that is right for you at this stage.

Some people choose a certain time of the day, and faithfully sit at that time, not allowing anything to interfere. People who meditate in the early morning normally find that it helps them to face the day in a calmer, more complete way than before, and it can help too in coping with the pressure and stress that we find in our normal daily routine. People who meditate in the evening find that being in the meditative state enables them to emerge from that state with a great sense of self and of serenity of spirit.

If it is possible for you to meditate twice daily, the benefits are immeasurable at many different levels.

All of the visualisations I have written take place in a lovely garden, filled with peace and serenity, where nothing can harm you. This garden is not an external garden, but one that lives inside each of us and is therefore easily accessible. It is somewhere you can go that is specifically yours. Prior to entering your garden, there is a Worry Tree where you can place your concerns and cares, and that enables you to enter your meditative state free from those worries.

When you close the gate behind you, you have entered the garden and its peaceful state. You will find that the serenity and peace that you find there will be reflected back into your outer world, enabling you to feel good about yourself and your surroundings. By sitting quietly, going into your inner garden, you can use the meditative state for healing your mind, your body, your spirit, or by sending rays of healing to others even when they are absent.

Visualisation & Meditation

Meditation means going within, listening to the inner or Higher Self, while visualisation means using visual pictures in the meditative state to create what you need in your life.

Meditation combined with visualisation can be a very effective way to actively develop images of what we seek and desire in our life. We may want to improve our relationships or family life, to improve our achievements at work or study, or to see ourselves being positive and healthy. Visualisation means putting thoughts and images into a more specific, vivid form, where we can actively work on the images, whether it be for our healing or to attain our life's desires. Visualisation enables us to create a scene or an image within ourselves that will not only have a positive impact on our everyday life, but that will be reflected into all areas of our existence. If our life is out of kilter, and if we learn how to bring our life under control through using meditation and visualisation, the flow-on benefit is one of good health.

What we are doing by combining visualisation with meditation is setting up a scenario that, if we have a strong enough belief in what we are visualising, can be played back into real life. Meditation is a beautiful way of harnessing these energies. It gives us peace and quiet as we settle, and our visualisation then enables us to create the images we would most like to have reflected back into our health and life.

I believe we can use my approach to meditation to visualise what we need to have in our lives, whether it be better health, strength, love of life or people, a happier environment, a better place of work, or better study skills. In such meditation we go to an inner part of ourselves where - by sitting quietly as our breathing slows and our heart quietens - we learn the answers to our troubles.

According to universal spiritual tradition, the power of visualisation is irresistible if properly implemented. Visualisation is the creation of completely clear, detailed images, with the aim of imprinting an idea on the astral sphere, which may in turn reflect upon the physical sphere.

If you have a strong enough belief in who you are and what you are doing, and you apply this to your visualisation, then why would it not happen? As long as your motives are pure, as long as you do not try to influence another's behaviour to your own advantage and their disadvantage, there is no reason why it will not work.

Meditation has helped me in many ways. During my periods of ill health (which I will discuss in further detail later), I was able to improve my health and change the course of events by meditating and using positive visualisation. I meditated deeply to rid myself of my illness, but I also had a strong belief that it was possible to achieve this. At the same time, I sought medical advice, modified my diet and altered my thinking. As a result the course of my illness changed.

The visualisations within this book are an aid to enable you to see your health improving by using positive imagery. For instance, **The golden bell** visualisation (p.121) takes you to a special glen within your garden where you receive healing rays from a beautiful golden bell that hangs suspended in the air. **The river of life and the rainbow** (p. 155) takes you down a river where some of your past experiences may be shown to you. Some of these may be experienced as positive, while others could be extremely painful. If there are painful memories, they need to be released. You can do this by observing them, without participation, as your simple wooden boat takes you down your river of life. You shall then be taken underneath your glowing rainbow - its healing colours shall fall around you, bringing peace and tranquillity.

Visualisation knows no bounds. Your mind has an endless capacity to see and experience, and to draw upon images that can be utilised in the meditative state. Do not restrict yourself in your imagery. Feel free to go beyond what I have written. Visualise whatever you feel can help with your own particular illness, to improve your sense of wellbeing and to bring you to the optimum glowing state of health that you desire and deserve.

When you are using meditation and visualisation, learn not to focus on your dis-ease, as most people do.

Focus instead on your health in order to improve it. See yourself being healthy, being active, glowing with health and vitality, being up and doing. The mind will accept that this is so and it will respond by improving your state of health and mind.

Karma

We often hear people speak about karma, its responsibilities and how it affects our lives. The word 'karma' is an Indian word and means 'cause and effect,' that is, every action causes a reaction. If you believe in reincarnation, then you will understand that you have incurred both good and bad karma throughout the various lifetimes you experienced prior to this one. Similarly Saint Paul wrote, 'Whatever someone sows, so also will they reap' (Galatians 6:7).

Reincarnation gives us the opportunity to perfect our soul. To do this we must face many things, such as love, hardship, richness, poverty, violence, solitude, birth, death - and all the things that human nature can and does experience. It is how we have dealt with the experiences in our previous lives that affects our current life. If you believe that who we are now is the sum total of our previous lives, then all of our past experiences have made us who we are today.

Many people wish to go back into past lives to find out what their experiences were. I think it is important that such people look at why they feel this need. If it is out of curiosity only, I query their need and I would not advise acting on it. However, if the past is impinging negatively on their current life, then they should give considered thought as to whether to do a regression.

Regression is where you are taken back by hypnosis or rebirthing into a past life. The therapist will endeavour to take you back to the life that has been causing the conflict or ill health in this life, in order for you to let the past conditions go. If you elect to be regressed, do choose a therapist who is well respected - it is very important that regression be done properly and well, for your own safety and wellbeing.

Another matter of prime importance with regard to regression is to remember that you are the observer and not the participant of the past-life happenings. By being the observer you remove yourself from the pain you may have experienced, and it gives you the opportunity to change outcomes. If, for example, you have continuous pain on the left side of the body that has bothered you for some time, you may find that you died through a spear piercing that side. To alleviate the symptoms that may be giving you discomfort and pain in this life, you could perhaps 'see' the spear turning into a wand of flowers, which would take away the intensity of the fear and pain associated with that particular past life. Although you cannot alter the past, you can change your vision of it, which will bring relief and understanding into your present life.

Tim was having flashbacks into a past life where his son (who is also his son in this current life) died in the desert. He was extremely distressed by these painful memories and found it difficult to deal with them. We did a session together where, instead of seeing his beloved son dying in the desert, Tim placed him on a grassy knoll underneath a beautiful arbor where deer and small animals grazed, and he then saw his child slowly and comfortably being absorbed into the earth. Tim learned to be the observer and not to participate in the pain he had experienced during that lifetime. This helped him in coming to terms with his past-life grief. Because of doing this past-life regression, Tim gained a different insight into his active three-year-old son, and this has also helped he and his wife enormously in dealing the boy.

We may want to believe that all our previous lifetimes have been blissful, that we have been spiritually evolved, generous and loving to all, but the reality is that many of these lifetimes would have been ordinary, some perhaps violent, with many involving relationships in which we were not always in the right. We may have murdered or been murdered, or been involved in wars or other conflicts. We would have given birth, loved many people intensely, and had many desires and wishes that were fulfilled, and many others that were not. If you believe that you are the sum total of your previous incarnations, then you must accept that who you currently are is the *real* you in this lifetime, the one who has experienced many things from the past, both good and bad, and that you have come back yet again to progress, to develop, and to overcome any negativity or karma from your previous lives.

Some illnesses may have a karmic origin or influence. Because karma means 'cause and effect,' what we have done in previous incarnations will have an effect upon our current lives. We may have treated our bodies unkindly in previous lifetimes, perhaps by indulging our bodies with excessive alcohol or food intake, or perhaps by living in a state of fear or negativity.

I believe that some people choose an illness as part of their life's work, as something they need to do and experience in the larger scheme of things. If you believe in reincarnation and in personal responsibility, you could well find the illness that you experience as being restrictive in this life, has come about because of your actions in a previous one.

If we could see the complete tapestry of our existence, in which all of the lives we have lived have been woven together, then we would have a better comprehension of the whys: 'Why am I the one who is ill?' 'Why should it be me?' 'I'm basically good and kind, why me?' 'Why do things happen to me that are out of my control?'

If we believe that karma enables us to pay off past debts, then we believe that we must go through learning or difficult times in order for this to occur. Illness may well be one of the ways of repaying a karmic debt, but because it is difficult to recall what has occurred prior to this lifetime, it can also be difficult to accept our illness. We do not have the overview to see our past mistakes or to know why we may have chosen to experience this illness.

There are some illnesses that will not be healed because they are not meant to be healed in this lifetime. Perhaps the experience of the illness is something that has been chosen so that we can understand how it feels to be dependent upon another's generosity and help, and to lose our independence. This illness may well be an opportunity for growth, and therefore we should bless this opportunity as being one given to us in order to overcome past karmic conditions.

Some people worry about incurring bad karma, forgetting they have attracted and are still attracting good karma by their positive actions. 'Love your neighbour as yourself' reminds us that we need to love ourselves totally if we are to love others. If we open up our heart chakra and allow the love to flow through for the self, then we can emit this love towards others. This obviously not only brings about positive karmic rewards, but a sense of feeling good about oneself.

We should live our lives in a positive way, knowing that we have the opportunity to learn as much as possible during this lifetime, which is the most important lifetime of all. Because we are the sum total of all our previous lives, from which we have learned and gained so much, then we should treat this lifetime as a journey of discovery.

The Aura

The aura is the energy field that surrounds the body, which for most people is invisible to the naked eye. The aura is up made from a collection of electromagnetic energies drawn from our physical, etheric, mental, emotional and spiritual bodies. This energy field emanates from our body and extends around it, giving the appearance of an oval egg completely surrounding us. Some people have an aura that extends quite a distance from their physical body, while the aura of others will stay close to their body. The more spiritually aware you are, the wider and more far reaching it becomes - the aura may extend for metres in all directions.

The aura is blended with many colours and is beautiful to see. The colours within the aura are similar to those of the rainbow, only perhaps more delicate or subtle. While some auras will reflect the beauty of these colours with their richness and vitality, others will appear to be quite dim, as though the lights have been turned down, muting their colours. There are varied reasons for this, such as how the person is feeling at that time, whether they are in a negative frame of mind, how their health is, whether they are joyous and happy, and whether they are advancing along their spiritual pathway.

Children normally retain their spiritual sight and images until around the age of seven, but as they settle into their school work and learn to do logical things, it seems the vast majority lose their spiritual vision. If a child starts to draw rainbows around people, they are seeing the auric field. Unfortunately, they are often told that rainbows belong in the sky after the rain clouds have cleared, which makes the children doubt what they have seen. Many people would have retained their spiritual vision if similar incidences had not occurred in their childhood, and would now be able to clearly see auras as an adult.

My daughter, Eleanor, used to see spirit people clearly and converse with them. When she was about ten, she was riding her bike on the footpath near our house. I looked out to see her talking, but an overhang of bushes blocked my view. When she returned, I asked to whom she had been speaking and received a negative response. I knew by the way she had been standing and gesticulating that she had been having a conversation with people who were hidden from my view, and I insisted she tell me. She became quite angry, and said, 'If you *must* know, I was talking to a *man, a woman, and two fairies*,' and stalked off to her room.

When Eleanor was quite small, she would sometimes have eight or nine spirit children sitting with her on the kitchen floor. She would not only introduce them to me, but continue to have lively conversations with them. As she became a little older, that changed. I would see her talking to them, making gestures, appearing to have strong eye contact, and she would wait for their reply before speaking again. When I would ask her to whom she was speaking, she would say no one was there. Perhaps the spirit children had said, 'Don't tell your mother,' which would be the typical comment of a child.

I believe her ability to see spirit people has changed, perhaps through not wanting to be different or because the logical or left side of the brain is now more in control. Perhaps later in life this ability will re-emerge, when she feels comfortable with it.

Most small children are receptive and have natural psychic and spiritual gifts. They have the ability to see the colours of the aura surrounding not only people, but also animals and plant life. Because they have this clear sight and ability to see auras as well as spirit children or spirit friends, such children are sometimes ostracised by their peers and their families for having this gift. Not everyone understands these things, so these children may be labelled as being strange, or daydreamers with their heads always in the clouds. They may close themselves off and stop talking about their ability to see auras or spirit people, as they want to appear 'normal' and be like everyone else. However they will often delve into the spiritual part of life at a later time, when they have a better understanding as to why their childhood experiences have been different to others.

Fortunately nowadays I believe people are becoming more aware of their children's gift to see things they themselves cannot perceive, and they do not discourage their children's ability to do so.

Your aura can change according to your mood, your emotions and your health. There are some people who can do health readings through their ability to see the aura and its colours, and they can see where the health problems lie within the auric field.

If you are not feeling well or your energies are down, sit quietly in the meditative state. Bring white light totally through your aura, so that this light will not only cleanse your aura and remove any impurities, but it will bring light and warmth into your being. This is a very simple exercise and you can go about it in several ways. One way is to see white light forming as a mist around your auric field, and then see it being slowly absorbed into it. Your aura will become brighter and brighter as this beautiful white light completely enriches and enlivens your auric field, which will help in healing your physical body. Another approach is to see a brilliant white light above your head, and then to bring this white light pouring through the auric field, washing and cleansing it, taking away any negativity or feelings that do not belong. Your aura then glows with health and vitality, which will be reflected back into your physical system.

Because our aura extends beyond the physical, we can attract those to us who have a similar or compatible energy field. We often wonder why we can feel angst towards someone or instinctively avoid them, while with others we feel an immediate affinity. Our aura pulls back if our energy fields are incompatible, and expands when we are compatible.

You may sometimes find that you are attracting people to you who have a need, and wonder why. These people are attracted towards the auric field of those people who can help them, and they instinctively gravitate towards them.

When I was socialising, I used to wonder why I was the one who would attract people with problems. I would be with a group of friends listening to music and one person after another, whom I did not know, would come to stand next to me, unload their problems, and then wander off. My friends used to laugh and ask what I was doing to attract so many diverse individuals with their various problems. Obviously they must have been attracted by my aura and, by telling me of their unfortunate experiences, it helped them get a different focus on what their problems were and how to bring resolution to them. The healing ability within the aura attracts many people who have a need to unburden themselves.

Kirlian photography was invented over fifty years ago by the Soviet husband and wife team, Semyon and Valentina Kirlian, who found that by using a high-frequency spark generator and normal film and paper, they could produce images different to anything that had been produced by using other methods. Their unusual photographic technique showed the energy field around various objects, including a leaf that had been cut in half, yet which appeared whole in the photograph. This was, and still is, an exciting innovation. They proved again and again that the energy field around objects did not change, even when the object was mutilated by slicing it in two, as with the leaf.

Kirlian photography enables us to see the energy fields surrounding not only inanimate objects, but also of people. If you place your hand on a special Kirlian photographic plate, the print will show the energy field around your fingers and palm. Some photographs will show a distinctly solid impression of energy sparks, while others will be quite light, but in each instance the energy field is shown.

It is interesting to note that when a person loses a limb, the amputee often feels the missing arm or leg still exists. They feel as though it is still attached and can also feel pain emanating from it. This shows the aura or energy field is still whole, even if the body is not.

When I begin a new meditation class, before taking them into meditation I get each person to extend their aura by pushing it out. I ask them to do this only from the right side of their body, so that it touches the person on their right, going from them to the next person, and so on, until it completes the circle and returns to the left side of their body. This is quite an interesting experiment. When you push the aura out from only one side of the body, it is as though you have drawn a line down through your centre, so that the side from which the aura has been extended feels warm and connected, and the other side feels cool and disconnected. I then get the group to go through the same process by pushing the aura out from the left side of the body, to bring them into balance. This is a simple exercise that I repeat for a few weeks when I take new people into my class, so that each of them can experience the difference between extending the aura on only one side of the body, as opposed to extending it equally from both. This increases our awareness of our body and its auric field. After people have had this experience and understand it, I revert to my normal way of extending the aura on both sides of the body to ensure that the group sits well as a whole, in harmony, and being connected by our energy field.

The Chakras

There are seven main chakras in the body. The term 'chakra' is a Sanskrit word meaning wheel, and these wheels are seen as spinning or rotating vortexes of energy. They are centres of force located within our etheric body and are aligned with the spine. The etheric body, sometimes referred to as a template, is a replica of the physical body and stands slightly removed from it. The chakras are doorways through which our mental, emotional and spiritual forces flow.

Bringing your chakras into alignment and cleansing them will result in a feeling of being more in control and assertive in your life. It also brings about a feeling of being connected with the God Force and the Universe, and brings the physical into line with the spiritual.

Each of the seven chakras is associated with a colour, and specific parts of the body resonate to that chakra and colour. However, this does not mean that you must restrict yourself to only using the colour normally associated with each of the chakras. Feel free to take through the chakra or chakras whatever colour or colours you are guided to use.

You may feel the need to work on the heart chakra in order to release emotion, to heal a recent hurt, or perhaps to deal with residual pain from years gone by that has not been internally reconciled. Although the colour for the heart chakra is recognised as being green, and indeed sometimes yellow, perhaps there is a need for *you* to work more with pink in that area. This may be explained by the fact that the heart deals with love and emotions and pink is allied closely with these feelings.

Violet is the recognised colour for the crown chakra, but you may feel the need to use white or gold light, in which case it is the correct colour for you at this time.

Allow yourself to adapt whatever colour of the rainbow appeals to you, and to take it into your chakras, or chakra if you are dealing with only one specifically. Do not hesitate or analyse why you feel that that colour is the one to be used, just do it. You cannot make a mistake – there is no wrong way.

Although there are other chakras within the body, including the hands and feet, the seven main chakras commonly referred to are:

Crown chakra

Situated: Top of the head.
Colour: Violet.
Functions: Upper brain, pineal gland, cerebral cortex, central nervous system, right eye.
Glands/organs: Pineal gland, cerebral cortex, central nervous system, right eye.
Qualities: Oneness with all that is, selfless service, spiritual unity, inspiration, wisdom, understanding, idealism.

Brow or third-eye chakra

Situated: Centre of the forehead, between the eyebrows.
Colour: Indigo (violet-blue).
Functions: Lower brain, sight, central nervous system.
Glands/organs: Pituitary gland, left eye, ears, nose.
Qualities: Clairvoyance, intuition, imagination, perception, insight, concentration.

Throat chakra

Situated: Throat.
Colour: Sky blue.
Functions:: Communication, expression, speech, sound, vibration.
Glands/organs: Thyroid, throat, mouth.
Qualities: Universal truth, honesty, reliability, loyalty, creative expression in writing, speaking and thought.

Heart chakra

Situated: Centre of the chest.
Colour: Green.
Functions:: Energises the physical body with the life force, blood circulation.
Glands/organs: Heart, thymus, lungs, circulation, arms, hands.
Qualities: Forgiveness, compassion, unconditional love, tolerance, openness, peace, contentment, harmony within and without, acceptance of self and others.

SOLAR PLEXUS CHAKRA

Situated: Above the navel, below the chest.
Colour: Yellow.
Functions:: Metabolism, digestion, nervous system, emotions.
Glands/organs: Pancreas, adrenals, stomach, gall bladder, muscles, nervous system, liver.
Qualities: Overcoming desire, control of the self, will, logic, authority, personal power, transformation, awareness.

SACRAL PLEXUS OR NAVEL CHAKRA

Situated: Lower abdomen to navel area.
Colour: Orange.
Functions:: Procreation, reproduction, sexuality, assimilation of food.
Glands/organs: Spleen, bladder, womb, ovaries, testicles, prostate, genitals.
Qualities: Tolerance, emotions, movement, desire, confidence, ability to work harmoniously with others.

BASE OR ROOT CHAKRA

Situated: Base of the spine or coccyx area.
Colour: Red.
Functions:: Life-force, self-preservation, instinct, vitality, survival.
Glands/organs: Spinal column, adrenals, kidneys, colon, legs, bones.
Qualities: Health, courage, stability, patience, being grounded, individuality, physical energy.

The diagram on page 43 shows the locations of the main seven chakras within our bodies. I have also included the chakras situated at the hands, from which the healing energy flows, and those at the soles of the feet, which aid both in connecting us to the earth energies and in grounding us.

There are several ways of opening your chakras for use, one of which is to start with the spiritual chakras, and then work down to the physical ones. I have always used this method because I have found that it is the one that works best for me. I begin by seeing a white rosebud appearing at my crown chakra, and then I perceive it as becoming larger and larger until it is a fully opened white rose. The beautiful petals of the rose are folded back, so that my crown chakra is fully open and aware. I then take the stem from the rose down to my third eye. There I repeat the process of seeing the bud becoming the rose until it is fully opened. I open each of the following chakras in the same way - throat, heart, solar plexus, sacral - until I reach and open the final one, the base chakra.

When I have finished meditating or working with healing, I then close the chakras down in the reverse order. I start with the base chakra and see the fully opened and aware rose closing its petals over and over, until it is no more. I then take the stem to the sacral chakra and repeat the process for it and each of the chakras in ascending order, until I reach the crown chakra. I close it in the same way, but with great care.

Another way of opening the chakras is to commence from the root or base chakra and continue up through the chakras, opening each one until you finish with your crown chakra. There are many people who prefer to take the light and energy *up* through their bodies, as they are then taking the physical energies from the three *lower* chakras (base, sacral and solar plexus) up to the four spiritual chakras (heart, throat, third-eye and crown). With this method, when you close the chakras down, then you should do it in the reverse order: closing off the crown chakra and then working your way through each one until you reach the base or root chakra.

Because there are these two different ways of opening and closing your chakras, you may like to try both ways on several occasions and see which one you feel the most comfortable with.

Your spiritual waterfall and chakras (p.110), **Cleansing your chakras with colour** (p.131) and **The wise old tree** (p.99) are visualisations I have written that deal specifically with the chakras.

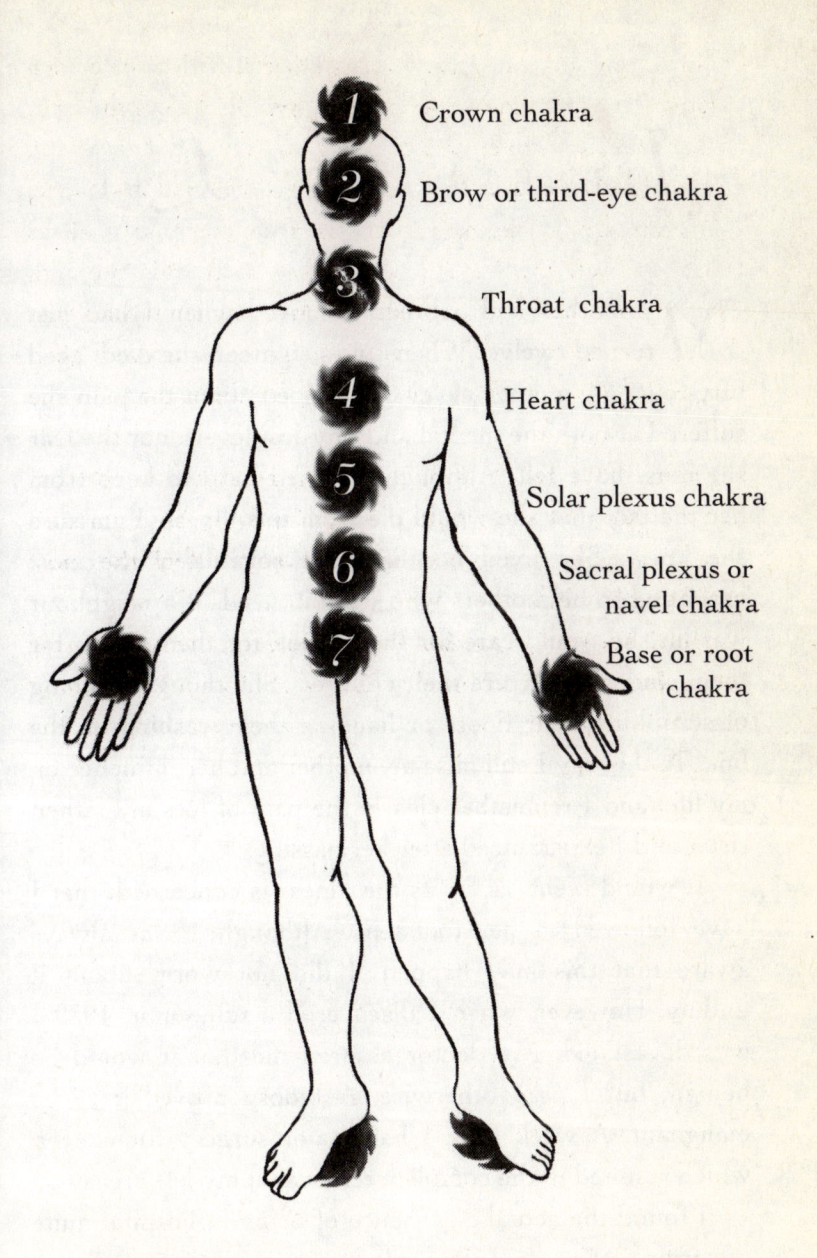

1. Crown chakra
2. Brow or third-eye chakra
3. Throat chakra
4. Heart chakra
5. Solar plexus chakra
6. Sacral plexus or navel chakra
7. Base or root chakra

Illness in My Life

My mother had a breast removed when I had just turned twelve. When I was eighteen she died, aged fifty-four. My mother never complained about the pain she suffered at both the mental and physical levels, nor the fear she must have felt. Although we tried hard to keep from her the fact that she would die from this illness, I am sure she knew. She lived her life in a spiritual way, never hesitating to help others who were in need. If a neighbour was ill, she would care for them, cook for them, clean for them, and also nurture their children. She thought nothing of scrubbing their floors or hanging their washing on the line. To this day I still miss my mother and her influence on my life, and I remember clearly the pain of loss my father, sister and I experienced after her passing.

It would seem, as far as the illness is concerned, that I have followed in her footsteps. Although I was always aware that this may happen, I did not worry about it unduly. However, when I discovered a tumour in 1979 I was devastated. My doctor assured me that it would be benign, but I *knew* otherwise. A biopsy proved it to be malignant. A week later I had major surgery for cancer, which resulted in the complete removal of my left breast.

I found the actual experience of being in hospital quite rewarding. The day after my operation, my first visitor arrived at eight in the morning, and people poured through the doors in support until nine that night. I had not realised that I had so many close friends and acquaintances, and I bless all who came. Without them, their love and their prayers, I may not have healed as quickly as I did.

Before leaving hospital, and while awaiting the results of my tests, I felt extremely depressed about knowing the outcome and I feared that the cancer may not have been totally removed. I decided to take a mental journey through my body, and, in doing so, I realised that the most important part of me was my eyes. I love to read, to watch people, to see the thoughts and expressions that form on people's faces, to see the sky with its fluffy white clouds, to see nature at her most glorious, to see the animals, and to see humankind, sometimes at its worst, more often at its best - whatever it may be, I just love to see.

Assessing my body in this way made me realise how little I had lost, and, importantly, it also gave me a very real sense of wellbeing. I received the test results the next day - they confirmed my own inner knowledge that the cancer had been totally removed.

I received many benefits from watching my mother's experience of illness. On the many occasions I went with her to the hospital for therapy, I never heard her complain about pain or what she was going through. She coped with her family and her illness, and she had remarkable courage and fortitude. I learned about courage from her, about persevering and getting on with life, and these lessons helped me enormously during the time of my own bout with cancer.

I rarely talk about my cancer, but when I have come across people who have the same condition, I have found my experience to be invaluable in helping that person. By writing about my experience, I am hoping that it will help others, not only those with cancer but those suffering other illnesses.

After the operation I found that I had inherited my mother's strength and capacity to cope with pain. This, plus my own sense of self, helped me to adjust. It is in my Sagittarian nature to be optimistic, and after the operation this part of my nature helped me enormously in my voyage of self-discovery.

The most wonderful outcome of my illness was the birth of my beloved Eleanor. Having had cancer, I could no longer take oestrogen and I fell pregnant the year after my three operations (biopsy, mastectomy and reconstruction). I bless my illness as something that brought untold benefits in so many ways. I cannot conceive of life without my beautiful daughter. Because of her advent into my life, she brought me a degree of joy and happiness that I would never have believed was possible. And it is because of my life experiences with her that I became a writer and a teacher of meditation.

When we go through a major crisis in life, whether it involve issues of health or personal loss, we generally do not know what other possible outcomes could have occurred beyond the expected ones, nor the long-term results. We may feel devastated at the time, but the end result could well be something positive that will give an added depth to our life. Perhaps the crisis is something that was needed in order to bring change into our lives, or to alter our thought patterns. But during the crisis, we are unaware of the knowledge and the strength we may gain from going through this experience, which appears at the time like a major catastrophe.

Prior to my hospital stays, I did not practise meditation. Between the time of my mastectomy and my reconstruction six months later, I went to meditation classes and found they brought me a lot of solace and comfort. I believe meditation not only aided the healing process, but also my understanding as to why this illness had occurred in the first place.

Perhaps if I had taken control over my life earlier the cancer may not have occurred. I had been working in an environment that was inappropriate for me and I felt terribly unhappy. I had a mortgage with the insurance company for whom I worked and, instead of moving on, I allowed the financial aspect to keep me anchored in a situation from which I really should have removed myself. I have learned that nothing is worth feeling that degree of stress over, and that you must take control over your life. If you are unhappy at work or at home, change your environment as it can have devastating effects on your life, including your health.

Through sitting in meditation I learned the benefits of healing and that we all have the ability to heal ourselves. This proved to be very beneficial when I became ill some years after my mastectomy.

I went through a terrible period where I was so ill that I was spending two-thirds of the day in bed. Being stubborn, I refused to go to the doctor. Eventually I reached a stage where I was sick of being sick. The doctor discovered that, in addition to a virus, I had a sizeable cyst in the pancreas. I went into an immediate state of depression at the thought of another operation, and I stayed in that state for several days. I then decided to do something positive about it.

On the physical level, I gave up tea, coffee, alcohol and fried foods. On the inner level, I meditated. Using strong visualisation, I saw the cyst becoming smaller and smaller and eventually disappearing through the elimination tract, until it was no more. I kept using meditation and visualisation each day, and, most importantly, I *knew* and never doubted that I would succeed.

Three months later I had another ultrasound and blood tests that showed that the cyst had disappeared. I was not surprised, as I had that inner knowledge that I would be healed. I had felt certain that by using the power of the mind in meditation and visualisation, my body would be healed.

There are many in the medical profession who agree that the body is controlled by the mind and that we do have the ability to heal ourselves. My local general practitioner is one of them. He is a wonderfully supportive doctor who cares deeply about his patients. He was not surprised when I said that I had been successfully combining the meditative state with visualisation in order to change the course of my illness.

To this day I do not drink tea, coffee or alcohol. I rarely have anything fried, but I do find chocolate difficult to give up as it is, to me, one of life's pleasures!

Both of these illnesses showed me I needed change in my life at many levels. In both instances, I *knew* I would regain my health and that neither of these illnesses would recur. I have been meditating now for many years and it brings me such pleasure, such comfort, and such a feeling of wellbeing of spirit.

Illness
&
Ian Gawler

*I*an Gawler is an inspiration to many people who have been ill. He has brought meditation and healing into his life with results that have amazed many people. Ian had bone cancer that was severe enough to warrant the complete removal of his right leg in January 1975. The following November he had multiple cancerous tumours pushing their way through the chest wall, and in March the following year his surgeon felt nothing further could be done for him. He was given only a few weeks to live.

Ian wanted to live, to be with his wife Grace, to have children and to see them grow. He accepted responsibility for his illness and by doing so felt in control. He became convinced that he could be cured, provided he took appropriate action. Importantly, Grace shared this view and together they embarked upon an extraordinary healing journey.

They did not accept it was Ian's time to pass over. Instead of giving up, they decided to seek help from many different sources. They investigated a variety of healing techniques and then adapted what they felt was right for

Ian into his way of thought and living. Ian meditated deeply, changed his food habits and reversed his cancer. This sounds very simple and easy, but Ian realised that the body can heal itself, and proceeded to find the best way for his own healing.

This shows how the power of the mind, or 'right thinking,' combined with meditation and correct foods, aid in healing the body.

Ian and Grace's initial misfortune has been a boon to many who have sought the Gawler's out. Through their knowledge and their experiences, they have helped many people to heal themselves. If we believe in free will and personal responsibility in all things, perhaps there is a sense in which Ian chose his illness in order to help others. Ian is the author of *Peace of Mind* and *You Can Conquer Cancer*, and Grace is the author of *Women of Silence*.

Taking Control

*I*n getting to *know* that you will surpass or have surpassed your illness, you need to really feel it deep inside, without any doubts. There is no easy way to achieve this 'knowing' and no correct formula to apply. Each person is an individual and will find their own way to accomplish this.

After my illnesses I had a major shift in assessing my body, looking at it and determining what was important. I also realised that my thought processes needed to change because I had been in a negative frame of mind, having worked in surroundings that were not conducive to 'positive thinking'.

'Positive thinking' is taking control of your life and getting rid of circumstances that bring you down. Why accept that you need to stay in your current job if it makes you unhappy? Why stay in your current relationship if it is less than fulfilling? Why stay in your current home if it is not what you want? Why stay in a home unit if you feel the need for trees and flowers around you? Why stay in a house if you feel you no longer want to mow the grass and tend the flowers? Change. Look at changing your circumstances to what your desires are.

When we become bogged down with details, and feel unhappy in whatever aspects of our life that need changing, our body's system becomes clogged and feels our downheartedness, our sadness. This can be reflected back to us in terms of bad or indifferent health.

You deserve good health - you owe it to yourself to feel at your optimum, being the best you can be. The mind controls all avenues of health and being. Look at your thought processes, find where they are out of balance, and change them.

I think everything is suitable to eat or drink, provided it is done in moderation. I do not believe you must give up the luxuries or pleasures you obtain from drinking or eating, unless it is your desire to do so. We should be able to enjoy a little of this, that or the other. It is only when we tip the balance that we end up being out of balance on the physical level, which in turn affects the inner person and can show up in our lives as depression or illness.

Healing & the Power of Prayer

Throughout the ages prayer has been known to bring unexpected results in healing, often amazing medical professionals whose diagnosis has been that either the patient would not survive their illness or that their health would not improve. However, times are changing and some doctors and hospitals have been undertaking scientific investigations into the power of prayer, in particular the effects of prayer on people suffering ill health.

In 1988, the San Francisco General Hospital launched a study on the power of prayer and its effect on its patients, and decided to run the program with 393 patients in its coronary care unit. The results of this study were published in the *Southern Medical Journal* in 1988. The hospital asked for volunteers to take part in the study and requested that they pray for patients they did not know. These volunteers were not allowed into the hospital to see the patients for whom they were to pray. They were not told to use specific prayers or any particular format. Instead, the volunteers were asked to send their prayers from a distance, and in the form with which each individual felt most comfortable.

A computer assigned 192 patients to the control group, who would be prayed for over a ten-month period by the home volunteers. The remaining 201 patients formed a group that would not receive prayer. This was a double-blind study, in the sense that the doctors, patients and nurses were all unaware of who had been chosen to be in the control group. The prayer groups were only given the first names of their patients, plus a brief description of their diagnosis and condition.

After the ten-month period of prayer, the hospital found that those prayed for required less therapy; they were five times less likely to require antibiotics; they were three times less likely to develop pulmonary edema; and none of them required endotracheal intubation, whereas twelve in the group that was not prayed for required mechanical ventilator support. Also very few patients died who were in the group that was prayed for.

Another double-blind study was conducted on ninety-six patients with high blood pressure, and this study showed a 'statistically significant improvement in systolic blood pressure'.

The following three cases studies were detailed in a television programme called *Sightings*, which was screened on ATN 7 in December 1995.

In Riverside, California, a six-year-old boy skated down the street where he lived, but accidentally went onto the road and was hit by a truck. The impact of the truck ripped him open from the navel across to his back, and by the time the ambulance and police arrived, he had lost four-and-a-half units of blood, which was half his body's capacity, while lying in the street. At the hospital, the doctors found the boy's entire pelvis was crushed and he had huge open wounds. These were extremely susceptible to infection, which could kill him. The doctors believed that even if the boy lived he might not be able to have children, that his ability to walk would be substantially impeded and that he might have to wear a colostomy bag for the rest of his life.

His family prayed for him from the moment he was taken by ambulance to the hospital, and they never lost their faith that prayer would succeed. As the doctors worked on the boy during this time in hospital, his family continued to pray and never gave up hope that by some miracle he would be restored to full health. And their prayers and their faith were answered. After six days the child was walking without a cast or pins, and he is now quite normal, playing football and still skating.

There are various universities in the United States of America - including Stanford, Harvard and Drake - that are conducting studies linking the power of the mind and the power to heal. They are applying scientific methods to see if prayer does make a difference, as has been done by the tests conducted at the San Francisco General Hospital.

In 1980, medical researchers in Oregon devised an experiment to test the power of prayer under controlled laboratory conditions. Research was conducted on tubes that were filled with yeast and then sealed. Half of the tubes were prayed over by volunteers to see if prayer would make any difference to their growth rate, while the others were not. Researchers were amazed at the significant difference of the growth rate in the tubes that received prayer, as opposed to those that had not.

Reverend Franklin Loehr's *The Power of Prayer on Plants* describes the positive effects prayer had on the growth of lima beans, sweet pea seeds and corn when they were watered with water that had been blessed by prayer.

There are many instances throughout history of the power of prayer, including cases of healing that have occurred through the use of prayer. Having faith that prayer can work shows that the human consciousness can do something that the brain alone cannot do. It reveals that there is a Higher Power or consciousness that receives the prayers being sent on behalf of a loved one. When absent or distant healing is being sent to a person in need, whether it be by family or friends, or by groups who have been asked to remit the healing, it is often sent as a prayer and this can be extremely powerful.

HEALING & GRIEF

When we lose people we love through death, we ourselves need healing at many different levels. Death has a sense of finality about it, and the feeling that we will never see or hear our loved ones again can be very distressing. We miss the physical contact, not being able to put our arms around them, hugging them, kissing them, and not being able to ring them up when we are in pain, or when something joyous has happened. We miss not being able to tell them we love them, as well as hearing those words repeated back to us. We miss the communication and just knowing that they are there for us.

When a parent loses a child, it can be very difficult to reconcile this with the need to continue on life's journey. It is always assumed that parents will predecease their children, and when it happens in reverse the emptiness can be unbearable. Many parents are finding this with AIDS, which has taken so many people. Sometimes it is not only their son or daughter who passes over, but also their child's partner. Even their grandchildren may be infected by the HIV virus.

I know of one mother who watched her beautiful son change from a healthy, happy person with a strong physique, to one who had shrunk in every way - except courage - after contracting AIDS. One month before he died, his wife passed away with the same illness. He suffered enormous physical pain from his illness, but he was also emotionally drained by the loss of his wife and his concern for his child. He worried about the outcome and wellbeing of their energetic and beautiful five-year-old daughter who is HIV-positive. He still believed he would live and struggled to do so, but it was not meant to be.

How sad for this small child to have watched both her parents deteriorate over her short period of life, and then to lose them at such a vulnerable age. How terrible for both families involved, to watch this couple die in what should have been their prime of their lives, to have them predecease their parents, and to know that the young girl is both motherless and fatherless, and may herself die. These families needed, and were given, a lot of healing through their friends who stood by them, loving them, caring for them and listening to them. Sometimes their silence helped when nothing else could be said.

My healing group sent healing many times to Danny and Jill (their names have been changed to protect the privacy of their families), to aid in the alleviation of their pain and suffering and, as their time came closer, to also help them with their passage to the other side. Healing can be given whether an illness is incurable or not, and these healing rays will help with pain and suffering on both the physical and mental levels. We also sent healing to their families to assist them with their own pain and suffering, so different from that of their children, but no less painful.

A close family friend had been giving Danny healing, and because she could not always be there, decided to make a tape for him. She used **The star prelude** that always prefaces my visualisations, followed by two visualisations from my book *The Inner Garden*. She selected **The easel** because he was an artist, but modified it to suit him and his particular style. She also included **Floating** to give him the opportunity to experience the feeling of being above the earth and water, and to be in peaceful surroundings. When he was in the final days of his illness, and his pain was extreme, his mother would sometimes play the tape ten times during the course of the day. She found that the peacefulness of it and the security of having his friend's voice talking him through, enabled Danny to cope with the pain better, to relax and to let go.

It is important to note here that it is better for a person suffering to hear the voice of someone they care about, or with whom they share deep love, on a tape intended to soothe them, rather than the voice of a stranger. You may feel that your voice is not good enough, but you will find that, because you have made the tape with love and your voice is familiar, it will help your loved one in many ways. The familiarity of the voice that they know and love can be of great comfort and solace.

Those who are left behind can find it difficult to come to terms with the loss of a loved one, and it is important that they too receive healing. This healing can be given by others either by their physical presence or their thoughts, or those grieving can themselves sit and meditate, which will bring them much needed peace. As they meditate, they could place themselves in a serene environment and then bring healing colours around and through them. Time is the great healer, but it is best to start to work on our healing at the time of our loss.

Losing children through suicide is heart breaking, and there are always the painful questions: Why? Did they really mean to do it? Was it planned, or was the decision made on spur of the moment? Unless a note has been left, or they have given an indication of their intentions, mental confusion reigns for those left behind. They do a lot of soul searching afterwards, wondering whether they could have changed the course of events. The grief for these parents is heartbreaking, as often they had no previous awareness that anything was wrong.

Losing children through cancer, watching the suffering they go through, and seeing the courage they have to continue their treatments, and then having them pass over, leaves a hole that is difficult to fill. Often parents and friends appear to cope well with the illness and do not allow the child to see their pain. When the time comes for this child to pass over, parents find it difficult to get on with everyday living, as visiting the hospital to see their child, or nursing their child at home, has been such a large part of their daily or weekly routine.

Losing children, brothers, sisters, friends or partners through misadventure can have an impact, and the shock waves and feelings of disbelief may continue for some time. We always believe accidents happen to someone else, never to one of our own.

Losing your partner, the person you have shared so many years and events with, the person you turned to, the person who knew you from the inside, is especially heartbreaking. There are always so many things left unsaid and we tend to chastise ourselves for our failure to say them, particularly the words, 'I love you'.

The loss of parents can be extremely difficult. The ones that have been with us since birth, who have nurtured and cared for us, who have loved us unconditionally, leave a large hole in our lives when they pass over, whether you are five, fifteen or fifty years of age. No matter how old you are, the loss of a parent can be devastating. My mother died when I was eighteen, my father when I was thirty-five, and although time has gone by and the pain has eased, my memories of them are clear and my love as strong now as it was then - and I miss them still. Time does ease the pain, but does not remove the memories and the sadness.

With people who had difficulties with their parents - perhaps with not being understood or with a feeling of being unloved - unless these issues were resolved before the parents' passing, then there will be no closure and their feelings of loss may be more difficult as a result. For such people it would be good to do a meditation on going back and looking at your parents when they were children. See them growing up, experiencing similar difficulties to those in your own life experience, and understanding that their path through life was not always easy. With understanding comes forgiveness, and in letting go of the pain, you will receive healing.

Some years ago I saw a friend of mine die with dignity and grace. Joy was a delightfully refreshing person who had travelled far and wide, lived overseas for some years and who had many friends from all avenues of life. Joy discovered she had breast cancer and dealt with her radical mastectomy in a positive manner. However, nine months later it was discovered that she had secondary cancer in the liver, which was pushing the liver across her stomach, and she was given only a short time to live. Not only did she find it difficult to eat but her breathing was affected by the tumour. One Saturday Joy held an open house at her home in order to say her farewells. All day, until late at night, people poured through her door with food, drink and laughter, and of course many of them cried after leaving.

I couldn't attend her farewell party, but Joy came to my house for lunch so that we could say goodbye. We spoke about many things, one of which was her anger at dying so young. She felt she still had so many things to accomplish, even though she had already done so much in her life. However, she thought it was a blessing that she knew her time was limited, and therefore had time to say her goodbyes. We spoke about her soul's envelope being discarded upon her passing and her spirit going 'to the other side' to be with other family and friends. We spoke of many, many things, and neither of us cried. She gave some of her beloved mementos to Eleanor and me, which we still have and treasure.

Joy died two weeks later, ten months after her mastectomy, at forty years of age. She showed courage during her illness and during the time she knew her death was approaching. She left behind many family members and friends who loved her deeply, and I am sure she is still remembered for her courage and her dignity. She spent her last few weeks being with those she loved, and having her going away' party was a great blessing. Allowing people to say their final goodbyes not only helped alleviate their grief, it helped begin their grieving process in a positive fashion.

How fortunate Joy was to have had the time to say farewell to those she loved and cared for. Not all people have this opportunity. We should remember to frequently tell our loved ones that we love them, that they are special and that we care for them in so many ways. Life can be short and we should ensure that our loved ones are aware of our feelings and that we do not leave it until it is too late. How many times have people grieved and worried because they did not say 'I love you' to their loved one prior to their passing, or that they did not make amends for past wrongs?

I do not ask that everyone believe as I do, but my belief is that when we die, it is only the physical envelope that dies, the body that has encased us during our time here on earth. I believe the spirit lives on, is eternal and never dies - so therefore there is no real death. I also believe that when our loved ones die, we can still at times feel their presence around us and communicate with them. Perhaps they are even more alive in the spiritual realms than when they were on this earth.

Yoko Ono was asked by a reporter how she felt after the death of her partner, John Lennon, seeing they had spent about ninety-five per cent of their time together. Her reply was, 'But how lucky I am, as now I have him one hundred per cent of the time'.

I believe that when people pass over, they go to sanctuaries where they receive healing and are given an understanding of why they chose that particular illness, or that particular way of death. Some may spend longer than others in these sanctuaries, depending upon the length and severity of their illness while in the physical body.

If you know of someone who has been experiencing the loss of a loved one, or who is preparing for loss, send that person, and those close to them, love and healing each night. It does not have to be lengthy, but a few moments of sending positive healing thoughts will help those grieving, as well as the person who is preparing to pass.

Words have strength and power, and it could well be that the words you use in comforting someone during their time of loss will have an enormous impact upon their grieving process. The power of thought is marvellous, and positive thought, even sent from a distance, will aid those who grieve, and will help you yourself in your own grieving process. Thought has power and thought travels.

Over the years I have come across several poems that I think greatly help those left behind to understand that their loved ones have gone on to a better way of life, and that they live on, regardless of having lost their physical envelope. One of these was written by Louis de Valdo Colosio, a Mexican presidential candidate, who was on a plane from Mexico to Valencia when he wrote the following poem for his wife in the early morning of 23 March 1994.

Think of Me

If you love me
do not cry.
If you know the unfathomable mystery
of the heaven where I find myself
you would never cry for me.
We loved each other eternally in life
but everything then was fleeting and limited.
Think of this marvellous place
where there is no death
and where I am near the inexhaustible source
of happiness
and love.
If you truly love me
cry no more for me.
I am at peace.

Colosio was assassinated later that day. He was obviously somehow aware at the time of writing this beautiful poem of his imminent departure from this life, and he did not want his wife to mourn. He wanted to reassure her that upon leaving the physical plane, he would go to a place where there was no death as we know it, and that he would be happy.

We who are left behind need to know that our loved ones have gone to a better way of life than they experienced while here. We can help in their passing by sending healing even after they have gone over. We can do this either through a visualisation in which we see them passing comfortably and happily to the other side, or by words of prayer. I visualise sending them white light, and I see them being taken up into the light where they are met and greeted by the loved ones that have preceded them. I see them glowing with health and vitality as they are taken on to the other side.

I have written several meditations, chiefly **Grief and loss** (p. 166) and **The Summerland** (p. 173), to aid in healing from grief. These meditations will not compensate for the loss of a loved one, nor are they meant to. They are intended to help you in the healing process of grieving. You may wish to adapt them to your own set of circumstances, or you may decide to use them as they stand.

Healing with Colour

In a meditative state we can look at the part of our body that needs healing and take colour through into the section that has 'dis-ease'. Bringing colour through the body is a marvellous way of altering energies and getting a better flow of energy within ourselves. Always take your time with each colour, so that you can feel the colour being well absorbed into yourself.

Before using colour, and in order to prepare your body for the healing, surround yourself with cleansing white light and take this white light entirely into your body, knowing that the healing has then begun. After doing this, select the colour you want to use. See the colour forming as a mist around your body, and then being absorbed into and through yourself. The colour you have selected will not only be taken through your body, touching each organ, but will be more concentrated in the area that requires healing. If you require a general, non-specific healing, the chosen colour will illuminate each part of your body with its healing properties.

Be guided by your intuitive self as to the colour or colours you need to take through your body, and you will use only those that your body, mind or emotions require. Don't confuse or worry yourself as to whether you have chosen the correct colour as the colour that comes to mind, or the one you 'feel' is right, is the correct one for you. You may feel a desire for a rich blue followed by a golden light, or perhaps a rich red to improve your energy levels, or you may feel the need to use all the colours of the rainbow. Follow your feelings and allow your intuition to come to the fore in the selection of the colours needed for your healing.

Blue is a wonderful healing colour, very gentle and restorative, and can be taken through the entire body to enable the body to begin its healing process. This colour will aid in cleansing the organs, or the other parts of the body that are in need, as it becomes absorbed into your body, bringing with it optimum health. There are many shades of blue that you can use - pale blue, sky blue, electric blue or even indigo. Look at the sky and bring its glorious colour through when the sun is high in the heavens, or when the light is fading and changes the blue to a gentler, more subtle colour.

Green is the colour of regeneration. It collects at the points where the body has been harmed or cut, allowing its colour to aid in the process of regenerating new tissue for those areas in need. Green brings strength and wholeness with it, and it aids in healing dis-eased tissues. You may want to see the green of the leaves of your favourite tree entering your body, or perhaps the green lushness of the velvet grass.

Red is ideal for taking through the bloodstream, the veins, the arteries and the heart, to rid the body of toxins, and to brighten, purify and energise your body. Red will assist in the issue of new blood, and in helping the blood supply to the heart, getting the heart pumping as it should be. If your energies are down, taking through a rich red will bring your energy levels up, so that you feel new life surging through your veins.

Yellow is great for the mind, bringing through clarity, purpose and drive, and enriching the brain cells. If you feel negativity within your mind, it is also good to take a pure golden light into that negativity in order for you to feel more positive and sure of yourself. Yellow and gold will strengthen and stimulate the mind, bringing clarification and a brightness that may be lacking.

Silver has the ability to enter and be used like a laser beam into those parts of the body that may be congested or closed up. If you find that your bronchial tubes are clogged, taking a silver light through them will help the passageways to clear. Silver also brings clarity and strength, and can be used to clear any obstructions that impair the body from functioning at its fullest capabilities.

Pink is a glorious colour to take into the heart, as it represents love. If love is lacking within, either for the self or others, ill health and dis-ease may appear within the body, heart or mind. Flood your heart with the pink of a glorious rose, or perhaps another beautiful flower that is special to you, and feel your heart changing as it receives this colour's richness.

Lavender is a delicate, pervasive colour that can highlight the need for peace and quiet within us. It can also gently deal with memories. Our minds are so aware, so receptive, so inclined to retain images that need to be put to rest. Taking lavender into this area will help you to understand the memories that are coming to the fore, and to then focus only on those memories that are positive.

Purple is the highest of the spiritual colours. It is a beautiful colour to bring around yourself after finishing your healing of the physical. It helps in combining the spiritual, mental, emotional and physical, so that your being works as one. You could perhaps see purple pansies or deep purple violets around you, and see yourself absorbing the colour from these flowers, feeling your understanding of the spiritual nature of the self coming more to the forefront of your consciousness than you have previously experienced.

There are many colours that you can use because all colours, except black, are good for healing. Remember to be visual and use imagery if you are not certain of your colours. See your own personal rainbow with its many glorious hues, and be guided by your own intuitive process as to what colours to choose and where to place them. See your garden with its plenitude and variety of beautifully coloured flowers and use their colours for bringing health and restoration to your body.

Blend the colours, make them your own, feel them, breathe them in, become one with these beautiful colours. Bringing colour through the body is a beautiful way of working with healing energies. Feel the colours pulsating through your entire person, bathing yourself in their beauty, absorbing them, feeling their delicate touch.

Some of the visualisations I have written use colour as the primary healing tool. Choose the visualisation that is appropriate to how you are feeling and what your needs are at the present time. You may care to select **Cleansing your chakras with colour** (p. 131), **Healing with colour** (p. 151) or perhaps **The pool, the lights and the dolphins** (p. 117), where rays of light change the colour of the water you are entering, depending upon your needs. A number of the other visualisations also make use of colour for healing, and you will feel guided in your selection of the appropriate visualisation for you.

Absent Healing

When we know people who need healing, we can send healing to them even if they are at a distance from us. They do not need to be in our physical presence for the healing to have effect. This is called absent, distant or mental healing.

Healing can be sent by an individual or a group to one or more sick persons and it will be accepted by that person if it is right for them to be healed. There are universal laws that cannot be transgressed. Not all people want to be healed. Perhaps their illness is karmic and it may be something they need to experience. Therefore when healing is sent, it must be understood that the sick person may or may not be able to accept it. If the healing is not required and the person to whom it is sent rejects it at the spiritual level, which is their right, that energy will be used elsewhere. Absent healing cannot hurt nor harm anyone; it can only help, provided it is sent in accordance with the universal laws of acceptance.

Absent healing can even be sent overseas to friends or others who may need it. It can be sent to countries where war has broken out and to areas where famine exists. The healing thoughts you send will also help all those who are dying in these countries, whether you are aware of it or not. Group meditation has the ability to change the consciousness of others, such as in warring nations or where there is other conflict. If we pour positive thought out to such countries, it will help alleviate the pain and suffering its people are experiencing. If more groups of people joined in meditation and sent healing rays to such places, we would have a more peaceful world.

I keep a 'healing book' in which people write the names of their friends or relations in need. During our class and after our meditation, we always send healing in absence to those who are in the healing book, as well as to others who may be in need, such as those in hospitals, in countries where famine exists, in nations at war, in orphanages, in psychiatric hospitals and similar institutions, and to people in jail and their victims, especially the victims of violent crimes.

We will often do a special healing, if requested, by visualising the person being in the centre of our circle, and take various colours through the person's body to help in the healing process.

In March 1995, we sent healing to a man who was suffering from Alzheimer's disease and who could not speak English very well. Unknown to this man or his daughter, the girl who requested the healing was herself dealing with cancer, and they were also unaware that she had requested that absent healing be sent. When she saw the family a few days later, the father said clearly, 'You have been given some healing too'. I believe the spirit can travel outside the body so that not only did he know of the healing being given to him, but also that their friend had received healing herself.

Absent healing can be very powerful when it is sent by a group of people who have meditated together and who then send healing energies to those in need. The leader of the group will be guided as to the colours that need to be sent to the various parts of the body of the ill person by mentally placing the body of that person in the centre of the healing circle. The leader then describes to the group the colours required to effect the healing.

Before we start our healing work I often see the patient as lying in the air - being supported by it and nothing else - and looking comfortable as he or she is suspended in space. I usually get my class to envisage the person while I describe their symptoms, sex, age and any other information I may have. I go into as much detail as possible so that each person in the group has a clear idea of what is necessary to accomplish the healing.

When concentrating on the person to be healed, I describe the colours that are to be taken through that person's body, which will vary from person to person depending upon their illness and how I am guided.

I often start with white light surrounding the body, which is then slowly absorbed through the pores of the skin into their body. This white light is cleansing and therapeutic, and prepares the body for the other colours to follow.

The colours used may depend on the illness the person has. You will be guided in the selection and use of the colours by the God Force or your Higher Self. There is no colour you can use that is harmful. All the colours of the rainbow are natural and beautiful. If in doubt, visualise a rainbow and select the colour that appears the brightest for the section of the body you are dealing with. As you move through the various parts of the body, you may find that another colour from your personal rainbow will become dominant.

Black is never used in healing, but you may see black or dark spots in the body. This will indicate to you that the body is not in harmony. You should then take a golden light into the person, to illuminate and remove this darkness from the body or the mind.

When working with colours for illness, the colours can change according to the illness. For instance, if you are working on a brain tumour, you may see that the light you are using is not very strong and wonder why. It may well be that you need to start gently with that particular colour, knowing that as you work the colour may become more intense as the patient accepts its depth. You may wish to use 'laser beams' of silver light when dealing with growths or brain tumours. You could visualise this laser erasing the tumour or growth, by entering each part of the growth and destroying it.

If a person has cancer of the breast, or a breast has just been removed, and they are receiving radiography or chemotherapy, you may find that as you take the light through them that the light itself emerges having changed colour. It may look muddy or dull. This would be because the light is absorbing the cancer as well as the damage done to the body by those therapies.

Whether you are sitting within a group or on your own, it is good to send healing in absence to those in need.

Endeavour to do so at the same time each evening, or on the same night each week. Start your own healing book, so that your group can add the names of people they are aware of who are in need. You may be surprised at how quickly the book becomes full! Our healing book often amazes us as, depending on the number of patients and the extent of the illnesses, it emits a strong odour. It is almost as though the book itself is absorbing the illnesses. At other times, the odour is still there but much lighter and more pleasant.

Never forget that you are only the vessel for the healing energies and not their source. All healing comes from the God Force. We link into the energy that comes from the God Force, in order to transmit the healing energy. Always ask for your healing to come from the God Force and that your spirit guides (or angels) lead you in the right direction with your healing. If your pride takes over, so that you feel that *you* are the one responsible for healing, without acknowledging that you are just the vessel for the energy, then your healing energies will become mediocre and you will not be able to help those in need. Also, as you progress, remember to ask that you gain a deeper understanding of healing, its energies and its ways. Although we would love to heal all if we were able to, we must realise that all healing comes from the God Force and the decision is made at that level as to whom will be healed.

How to Give Spiritual Healing

The desire to heal can be extremely strong in some people and, if this is so, they will be led in the direction of healing by circumstances or coincidence (although probably better understood as synchronicity), until they realise that it is the right path for them.

Some people are natural healers and have great abilities to heal. Matthew Manning, author of *The Link*, and Betty Shine, author of *Mind to Mind*, are two of England's top healers - the results they have had with their patients have been nothing short of miraculous. It would appear that their destiny was to heal and that they could not escape that destiny, even if they had wished to do so. Matthew had many remarkable events happen to him at an early age, as a result of which he went through some years of scientific tests that eventually showed that science could not completely evaluate his gifts. Betty had an unusual life and came into healing after rearing her family. She evidently has the ability to change deformed or arthritic bones back into their natural state. Both Betty and Matthew give service to others through their healing abilities.

There are many good healers who will never be as well known as Matthew Manning and Betty Shine, but the work they do is perhaps no less exceptional. Healers normally give of their time freely, and in Britain and Russia it is accepted that a patient can ask for a spiritual healer to attend to them while in hospital. Perhaps one of these days this approach will be equally accepted in other countries, and spiritual healing will be embraced in the same way that medical healing has been.

You may feel guided towards giving healing to some family members or friends who are in need. I am sure you will be surprised at the results. If your desire to give healing is for the benefit of the other person, and not for self-aggrandisement, then you will find that the healing energies will flow. There are healing groups available where you can learn about energies and how to distribute them so that the patient feels the full benefit. If you are ready to heal, then the old saying, 'When the pupil is ready, the teacher appears,' will undoubtedly apply.

Spiritual healing is normally given to the patient while they sit on a comfortable chair, if a massage table is not available. It is necessary for the chair to be straight-backed, so that the patient's feet reach the ground. If the patient is not tall, their feet may dangle, which will be uncomfortable for them. If so, then you could put a small footrest or a telephone book underneath their feet for support. If you need to work on their back, the patient will have to sit sideways on the chair or, alternatively, you could place a pillow on their lap and get them to lean forward. This will enable you to work more easily on their back without strain. If you have a massage table, then you will be able to move freely around the person requiring healing.

Healing energies flow through our hands and our heart. Therefore stand behind your patient, placing your hands on their shoulders and allow a little time to elapse while you feel the energies coming through. Not only are our seven main chakras activated by this energy, but the chakras in our hands and feet will also be open and receptive. Energy works on different levels and may be experienced by the healer, and the patient, as being either warm or cold. As it comes through the hands, the energy is normally warm or exceedingly hot, and the recipient will feel this energy flowing into the areas that are in need.

I find it interesting that sometimes I can feel the warmth of these healing energies, and yet the recipient may feel the energy as being cool. Conversely when I am using a cool energy, the patient may experience it as being hot. It seems to become transmuted from the healer to the patient. Moreover there are times when you may feel the energies are light, but the patient feels the energy as being extremely strong.

This reminds us that it does not matter how we, as the healer, feel. We are not the one guiding the energy through the vehicle to be healed. The God Force does this.

I always open myself up to the God Force and ask that I work with energies that are only of the highest and the best good. Because I believe in working with spirit guides or angels, I also ask that they come forward to aid in the healing that is about to be given.

Spiritual healers offer themselves as the vehicle through which the healing travels, knowing they are but the conduit for this energy and not its source. We all have the ability to offer this energy to others and to aid in their healing process.

It is also important, after giving healing, to always 'close yourself down,' to thank the healers on the other side of the veil for their efforts in the healing undertaken, and also to thank the God Force for allowing us to be used.

You can close yourself off from the energy you have been working with in the following way: after sending your thanks into the Universe, visualise bringing down a beautiful golden cloak and wrap yourself in it. I always see mine above my head; it is made out of very fine chain mail, with an intricate pattern through which nothing can penetrate. Bring the cloak down over your head and shoulders, and take it down and around your body until it goes underneath your feet. This is an effective way of closing yourself off and sealing your aura.

Having an Open Mind Like a Child

My daughter, Eleanor, did healing as a child while at her infants school. At various times some of her fellow children in Grade 2 would feel unwell or have a headache. Eleanor would tell them to sit down and that she would heal them. She would put her hands on their head, back or chest, depending upon the source of the discomfort, and send healing energy into the part of the body that needed to be healed.

Eleanor had seen me giving spiritual healing to others, so it was natural for her to also give healing. I was quite unaware of how much she was taking in from watching me using healing energies, but it made me realise how much children always imitate and learn from their parents or teachers.

I was surprised when Eleanor first told me how she had healed some of her class mates and that she had told her teacher. I wondered how her teacher, Helen, would react to this, being a little concerned that she might think I was a 'nutty' parent and that this may reflect upon my child. I am well aware that not all people understand about this approach to healing. However, I need not have worried. One day Helen took me aside to ask me to teach the children how to meditate, and she brought up the fact that Eleanor had been healing the children. She commented that she had no doubt that the children were healed through Eleanor.

I am using this story to illustrate that healing can be given irrespective of who the healer is. Fortunately children are open and receptive in both giving and receiving healing. If we were to learn to be more child-like in the way we give and receive, then we too would have the opportunity to become healers as well as to be healed. If we can accept without question and preconceptions that all healing comes from a source outside of ourselves, then we too will trust like a child and be able to use healing energies for the benefit of others and ourselves.

Children do not put obstacles in their way as adults do. Adults become too concerned about how it should be done. Am I standing the correct way? Am I handling the energy correctly? I cannot feel the energy - perhaps I have none! Adults have doubts as to their abilities whereas it should be so simple.

Children readily accept or give healing because they do not have preconceived ideas about what healing is. When they hurt themselves and their parent or friend put their arms around them, their soothing touch calms the pain and anxiety that the child has been experiencing. When the parent is in pain, whether it be emotional or physical, they may find their child putting their arms around them and saying, 'It's OK, you'll be better soon,' and invariably you are. Eleanor has often sensed when I have had such a need and has given me healing without my requesting it.

We are not a touching society, which is most unfortunate. We learn early in life to be careful of people outside of those we know and love, and therefore we may find it difficult to place our hands on the shoulders or bodies of others. Most people who are new to my classes find this is so, and it takes several weeks before they begin to feel comfortable with the energies and the placement of their hands. Children, on the other hand, do not hesitate to go to the source of the discomfort and are accepting of each other, which again illustrates that we can learn from our children.

Because the source of the healing is a Higher Power, and because you are offering yourself up as the instrument for that healing, how can it possibly go wrong? It is not up to you to heal, only for you to be the conduit through which the energy will pass to the person who needs the healing. The God Force is the one which determines who shall be healed. Obviously if we could, we would heal everyone that came to us. That is not possible and it is not within the realm of our choice or responsibility to be able to do so.

Be like a child and have faith in your abilities. Ask to be guided and listen to that guidance for yourself, as well as for others.

Using the Visualisations In This Book

The method of meditation I present in this and my earlier books makes use of visualisations. The first of the visualisations I have included, I have called **The star prelude** (p. 97). It is used at the beginning of meditation, before the other visualisations, as a means of entry into the garden in which all my visualisations take place. I ask that as you sit you see a star above your head, and bring its light down through your body until you are filled with this light. Before entering the garden there is a Worry Tree, which is important because it helps you to enter into your meditation with a clear mind. Use the Worry Tree to put behind you any concerns you have, whether they be about family, work or friends, or any other pressures you are finding difficult to deal with. You may need to have meditated in this way a number of times before you discover how you can really use the tree to its fullest advantage, but this method does work and it works well.

It is also good to open up your heart and fill it with love, because we all need to learn to love freely and openly without requiring love in return. In other words, to love unconditionally. It is equally important to fill your heart with love for yourself, as sometimes we neglect to love ourselves. You may also want to feel the wings of an angel wrapped around you or perhaps imagine there is a wise person or protector with you. No matter how old we are, we need such security. At the end of your meditation, when you come back from the garden, wrap yourself in your golden cloak and send your energy back into the Universe to be used for the highest and the best purposes.

Each of my visualisations take you into your own beautiful inner garden, where nothing can harm you, where everything lives peacefully together, including the animals, and where nothing ever dies because there is no death.

After you have used **The star prelude** and closed the garden gate behind you, you can choose any of the visualisations in this book or draw upon images from your own mind. That is how it has always worked for me. There is no right or wrong way. You may visualise one thing and it leads to another, taking you in a different direction, or you may care to take the theme or images from one of my visualisations and develop them in your own style.

Meditation is very simple. You can begin by sitting quietly, either on your own or with a group of people. It is best to sit in a straight-backed chair - if you make the chair too comfortable, you may fall asleep. For comfort try to wear loose clothing, but if that is not possible loosen anything that is tight around your waist or neck so that you do not feel them being restricted. It is wise not to cross your arms and legs as this can also lead to discomfort.

You might like to have soothing music in the background or perhaps you might prefer silence; it is up to the individual and their preference. I generally prefer silence but I have occasionally meditated with music and have been happy with the experience.

Normally I go into the meditative state by going into my beautiful garden, where I have had so many good experiences, but there are times when my mind is like a blank screen ready to receive whatever images happen to cross it. Do not have expectations of yourself that may be difficult to fulfil - simply allow your inner self to guide you.

The brain works at different levels of consciousness. These levels are called Beta, Alpha, Theta and Delta. Beta is the normal conscious level, our awake state, the level at which we work in our daily lives. When we go into a meditative state we are going into Alpha, the state that enables us to create scenes and images on the screen of our mind. We can attain Theta as we go more deeply into the meditative state. Delta is our sleep level. In meditation most of us work very well within the Alpha level and come back feeling refreshed and renewed.

It is up to the individual to decide how long to spend in meditation. Normally if you can only spare five or ten minutes that will be ample. However, to feel the full benefit for healing, perhaps twenty or thirty minutes twice a day is better, because it is your meditative state that induces the healing energies. If you are well and do not especially require healing, meditation can promote calmness, relax tension, and give relief from anxiety as you become detached from your problems. Your problems will not necessarily go away, but meditation can help in the way you handle those problems. In fact sometimes the solution comes to you while you are taking the time to sit quietly in meditation.

Perhaps some of your attitudes have become negative through lack of direction or difficulty in expressing your innermost feelings and thoughts. You may think things are more difficult than they are, but if you find a new perspective to your problems, they may be easier to resolve.

The visualisations in this book are not just pleasant imagery. They are positive tools to be used in allowing your body, mind and spirit to work with healing energies. These meditations will encourage you to use healing in a positive way, whether it be helping you to deal with grief and loss, to receive healing from crystals, to send healing to others, or to cleanse the earth.

All of my visualisations are rich in images and take place within your personal garden, a garden where nothing can harm you, where there is peace and tranquillity. You will feel the warmth of the sun caressing you and will hear and see the flowers and the grass growing. Open yourself up to the experience, so different each time you enter the meditative state. Your garden exists within you and is always accessible.

In your garden perhaps you may have a golden lion to accompany you on your journey, or butterflies to fly before you, taking you further down your pathway into areas of your inner garden that you may not have encountered before.

Many of the visualisations are to relax you and to encourage you to 'see' more for yourself. They may nourish 'the child within' and allow you to feel nurtured and protected. All of them reflect healing at some level, and you may find that particular ones appeal to you at certain times of your life. Let the visualisations waft over you and allow yourself to relax into them. Each visualisation is different and should not restrict you in any way. Flow with them, enter into them, enjoy them. Appreciate the newness of each experience and accept it as bringing a positive energy into your life.

All of the visualisations in this book can be adapted to each person's individuality. You should be flexible about how you use them, feeling free to alter those visualisations you select to suit our own particular personality and problems with health.

The **Healing with colour** visualisation (p. 151) shows how you can concentrate on bringing colour into those areas of your body that need healing. As we have already discussed, meditation using colours and visualisation is a great aid in the healing process.

The stars and the miniature waterfall (p. 145) enables your spiritual self to feel refreshed by the buoyant waters, while the lights from the stars and the moon aid in aligning your emotional being.

The healing sanctuary (p. 177) is in a beautiful glen where angels come to give you healing.

Look at the visualisations listed in the table of contents and one title will stand out from the rest. Do not restrict yourself to what I have written. Feel free to change and adapt the visualisations to suit how you feel and what your needs are at this moment.

Meditating In Groups

I have taught meditation for many years. When I am teaching a group, I invite them to sit in a circle on straight-backed chairs, relaxing body and mind, loosening any tight clothing and taking off shoes if necessary. Although it is not mandatory, it is a good idea to remove any jewellery that may make a sound and to avoid strong perfume or aftershave. These can interfere with others meditating whose senses are heightened or who may be allergy prone.

A meditative reading of **The star prelude** (p. 97) begins the meditation. I then use one of the visualisations to lead the group to a place where I leave them to their own visualisation/meditation for a period of approximately forty-five to sixty minutes, depending upon how settled they are and how I feel. The length of time is up to the group leader - if you feel half an hour is sufficient, then that is the right length of time for you and them. When the group is new, it may be best to start with a shorter time, such as thirty minutes, and to gradually lengthen this as the group becomes accustomed to you and the art of sitting in the meditative state.

When I bring the group back from the meditative state, I do so from the place in the visualisation where I left them. I then take them back along the garden path to their gate, close it behind them firmly, and tell them to open their eyes when they are ready.

Some people settle more deeply than others into the energy that comes from sitting in a group, and they may take longer than others to come back. Sometimes when we go very deeply, we may want to stay in the energy and be loath to return. If the leader feels someone is staying in the meditative state for too long, they should call the person by name and tell them it is time to return. Life beckons and goes on, and so we must come back into the physical state.

As part of the visualisation I wrap each person up in a lovely golden cloak, to close them off from the meditative state. I bring this beautiful cloak down over the top of their heads, wrapping it around their bodies until it comes below their feet, before sending the energy back into the Universe to be used for the highest good.

If you decide to meditate as a group, it is important that you feel comfortable with each other. Sitting with someone who makes you uncomfortable can interfere with your meditation. However, I am sure that if you decide to set up a group, you will have only those with whom you are compatible. Choose a day and time suitable to all and keep to that time schedule. Do not allow other things to take you away from your weekly meditation group. Consistent attendance will bring many benefits to all of you. When sitting in a group, you will find that the group energy can make it easier both for you to enter the meditative state and to see things when visualising.

There must be one person to lead the meditation. Normally it is best for the same person to lead the group each week, but you could perhaps take turns. Such rotation gives leaders a chance to hone their own visualisation or imaginative skills and to make each meditation entirely their own.

The person who leads the meditation will not be able to meditate as deeply as perhaps they would like. They have to be aware at all times and able to bring the others back at the appropriate time. If the leader drifts off too far, who will bring the group back?

You might think, when you read them, that the meditations are not very long. Please remember that when you are speaking to a group, you will do so in a very slow, relaxed voice, pausing to let the scene sink in. Then the group, sitting with eyes closed and focusing inward, can easily visualise and enter into the scene. The way leaders use their voice is very important. It is best to drop your voice by a few tones and to speak more slowly than you are used to, with a soothing quality. There is a hypnotic quality about a low and relaxed voice that helps people move into the meditative state.

Meditating Alone

If you will be meditating by yourself, decide whether you prefer to meditate in the early morning or late evening, or both - indeed any time that suits you and when you are unlikely to be interrupted. Make yourself comfortable and relax, but first take the phone off the hook and do not have anything going on in the kitchen that will sound alarms. You do not have to meditate for long periods of time. However, if you are the type of person who goes in the meditative state very deeply but must be strict about your time, then fix a return time firmly in your mind. Generally you will find that you will return at the appropriate time. Alternatively you could set your radio alarm to music.

Even if you are alone, begin with **The star prelude** (p. 97), taking the light from the star down through your body. Work on your heart, leaving your worries on the Worry Tree, joining the wise person or guardian angel, and then going into one of the other visualisations. Read the visualisation through to fix it in your mind. Then sit and relax and let your mind ponder the selected visualisation, perhaps changing it to suit your personality or how you are feeling at the time. When you come back, please remember to wrap your golden cloak around you and send the energy you have been using back into the Universe for the highest and best good.

Making the Visualisations Your Own

Let me give you a final reminder that what I have written, be it **The star prelude** or any of the visualisations, has been written only as a guide. You may make any of them your own. Perhaps by doing so you will bring to mind details that I have not included. Don't restrict yourself - allow your imagination to roam, to be free and to bring into mind all the delightful aspects that appeal to you and help you to feel better within yourself.

Allow the healing to commence.

Part Two:
The Visualisations

THE STAR PRELUDE

I want you to see above your head a beautiful, beautiful star that is filled with white light, lovely white light that shimmers and glows. I want you to see this light streaming down towards you, until it reaches the very top of your head. Now I want you to bring this pure light down through your head and take it right down your body until it is filled with this glorious white light.

I want you to feel the light going down your arms, right down, until you feel it reaching your hands and going into each and every finger.

Now feel the light going down the trunk of your body, down until it reaches your legs. When you feel it there, take it right down until it comes to your feet, and then feel the light going through each individual toe.

Once you have brought this glorious light down, you are a beacon of light and have become as a living flame.

Look into your heart and fill your heart with love for all people and for all creatures, great and small. Can you see your heart getting bigger and bigger? It is expanding because you have so much love in your heart for all people, the animals, all living things, and of course for yourself.

Before you enter your garden, I want you to look at the large tree outside. This tree is called 'The Worry Tree'. I want you to pin on this tree anything that might be worrying you - perhaps you have problems with your work, or maybe you are having difficulties in your personal life. This tree will take any worries at all, no matter how small or how large. This tree accepts anything that you wish to pin or place on it.

In front of you there now is a wise person who has been waiting patiently for you to come, who will always care for and protect you. Can you feel the love emanating from this special person towards you? Or perhaps you have a guardian angel who will wrap golden wings of protection around you before taking you into your garden. The angel's wings are very large and very soft, just like down.

Everyone has their own guardian angel or wise person who takes care of them and protects them always, so remember that you are never alone. It is important to keep this is mind and to know that you have someone who looks after you with love and care.

Take the hand that is extended, open the gate before you and enter your garden, closing the gate firmly behind you. As you do, the colours spring to life, colours like nothing you have seen before. The beauty of the flowers, the colours, the textures and the perfume - take them all in. The grass is a vivid green and the sky a beautiful blue with white fluffy clouds. It is very peaceful in your garden - it is full of love and harmony.

The Wise Old Tree

Your garden is peaceful and quiet, so quiet that if you listen carefully you can even hear the sounds of the insects moving through the leaves that have fallen to the ground. The light breeze that has sprung up is stirring these leaves, rustling them, and their sound is like music. The billowing white clouds stand in relief against the clear blue of the sky, forming faces and shapes that look like animals, or perhaps even people you know or have known.

Lift your face towards the sun's light and feel its warmth as the gentle breeze moves like fingers through your hair. The sunlight dapples the pathway you are on and butterflies fly in front of you, leading you deeper into your garden. Some of these butterflies have huge wings for such small bodies and they reflect all the colours of the rainbow. Their beautifully patterned wings create a kaleidoscope of colour as they weave their way in front of you, showing you the way to the Grandfather Tree.

Follow them along the winding pathway that takes you to a clearing full of flowers of every description. The colour of the open roses bursts forth, while the small buds of other roses feel the warmth of the sun gently opening them. The white lilies reach for this warmth, as do the small patches of violets and the myriad of other flowers that live and thrive in your special garden. Towering over all the flowers, bushes and trees is a magnificent old tree whose branches are full and hang heavy with brilliant green leaves that move gently in the air. His roots reach out from his trunk, going deeply into the surrounding earth, pushing up from the earth and making mounds that appear like seats comfortable enough to sit on. This tree seems as though he has been here forever, and that time has stood still while he absorbed knowledge and wisdom from the air, the sky, the earth and all that lives.

This old tree stands tall and serene, as though he is the sentinel within your garden, always watching, waiting and caring for you. He is the Grandfather Tree, and the wisdom of the ages has been absorbed through his bark and leaves into his core, allowing this magnificent tree to stand tall, free and unfettered, reaching for the blue of the sky and its passing clouds. This tree is very old and very wise and it seems that he will live forever.

You feel as though you would like to stand with your back against the rough bark of this old tree's trunk. As you do so, you will feel the strength and the age of this marvellous tree permeating you and experience feelings of peace and tranquillity entering your body. Stay there for as long as you like, and feel your spine not only being strengthened but lengthened, as the energies of the tree aligns your own energies while working on your spine.

Put your arms around the Grandfather Tree's thick trunk and you will experience a great feeling of comfort as you do so. You will find the tree's strength and energies will not only work upon your spine but also your vertebrae and ribs, helping to remove any pain and discomfort you may have. You will notice that feelings of peace and serenity enter you. As these feelings grow you become aware that they are equalising and changing those parts of your body that are in need. You feel your heart expanding with emotion, allowing you to acknowledge your feelings, your sense of truth, your sense of self. Your heart and your mind seem as though they are now as one, working together in harmony, bringing peace and serenity to your inner core.

Stay for a period of time with your arms around the trunk of this glorious tree, or perhaps with your back against his rough bark, acknowledging and accepting the feelings of comfort and serenity you now feel, as a major shift occurs throughout your body. You can also feel your chakras being brought into alignment by the strength and energy of the tree. Feel yourself absorbing these energies, taking them through your chakras, cleansing and balancing them, making you feel centred and whole.

Feel the peace and tranquillity that resides in your special garden surrounding you. This peace and tranquillity is always there for you. You can feel it entering your heart, entering your body, entering your soul. You can feel it being absorbed into your body, into your very self, into your spirit, and you can feel your life force becoming free and open.

Feel the strength from the tree entering your body, bringing about the healing that is necessary, calming your inner person and strengthening your sense of purpose and destiny. Know that like the tree, you have innate wisdom and knowledge, that your roots are strong and secure and will support you always . . .

A Basket of Crystals

Your garden is beautiful and peaceful, and everything that grows and lives within your magnificent garden glistens in the light that is streaming through the trees. The sun hangs like a beautiful golden ball overhead, and the blue of the sky is enlivened by the wispy white clouds that drift across it. The trees seem to drowse in the sun's light, sleepily allowing the light breeze to ruffle the heavy leaves that engulf their branches. The flowers are sitting proud and tall, and create a kaleidoscope of colour that cascades throughout your garden, brightening the green of the grass and the surrounding bushes.

Your pathway is taking you underneath the huge trees that send shade to the smaller plants beneath. They stand as sentinels as you pass beneath them, and the sunlight sends small beams of light filtering through their branches as though to show you the way to the clearing that is ahead. You can hear the call of the birds as they sing not only to each other but to all those who care to listen. You feel as though you would like to become one of the birds and experience the freedom of their flight. Feel your feet lifting off the ground and your body being supported by the air as you follow their sound. They are flying ahead of you, taking you to the clearing, which is surrounded by trees, by the small bushes and other plants that intertwine around their roots, and by the flowers that thrust colour towards the sun's light.

Sitting in the centre of this clearing is a large silver woven basket. The sunlight is catching on its contents, sending light sparkling and reaching out in all directions. You come to rest at the edge of the clearing, but begin walking towards the basket. Feel the softness and the warmth of the grass beneath your feet, until you reach the basket. It is heavy and intricately woven, and the silver of the basket glows with a special light of its own. When you look within, you will see that it is filled with every crystal imaginable, of all descriptions and sizes, and in every colour. These crystals are filled with beauty. Their colours not only reflect the light from the sun but have also gathered within them the colours of the trees, the flowers, the bushes and the other plants. The sun's light reflects this myriad of colours into all corners of your special garden.

Each of the crystals within the beautiful silver basket can be used in your healing process, whether it be physical, emotional or mental. They have healing powers that will reach deep within you, bringing solace and relief.

You will instinctively know which is the crystal that you need at this time. You will notice that one of the crystals has gathered more of the sun's light than the others, or you will be attracted to it because its facets are so beautiful or reflect colours or images that are special to you. At other times you may wish to simply place your hand inside this glorious basket, and the appropriate crystal will then fall into your palm.

Perhaps this time you may wish to choose the crystal by the shape and colour that appeals to you. You will select the right one by your intuitive process, being guided by the inner self to choose what is right for you at this given point in time. Have no fear of making mistakes, as no mistakes can be made by your choice. Whichever crystal you choose will be the right one for the healing that you need to receive at this time, whether it be physical, emotional or mental.

Sit comfortably by the basket with the crystal you have selected. Allow the light and energy from this crystal to enter your mind, your body, your soul, your being, your spirit, and feel the healing that is taking place.

If it is physical healing that you require, apply the crystal to the part of your body that is in need. Feel the crystal's light and energy strengthening and energising your body. Feel this light and energy intensifying as it revitalises each organ within your body. Feel it cleanse your blood supply and sweep all toxins away. Feel a surge of energy and life-force rushing through your body as the light from the crystal connects with all the parts of yourself that are in need.

You may now feel that you would like to receive emotional or mental healing. You can do this by using the beautiful crystal that you have been using for your physical self, or you may wish to choose another. Hold the crystal of your choice in your hand and feel the energy from the crystal calming and soothing the part of the self that is need, allowing the healing to commence and to continue.

Feel the light entering your heart and your mind, bringing peace and tranquillity. Feel the peacefulness of your emotions and the strength of your mind and thoughts, and feel how whole you are becoming - physically, emotionally and mentally.

This silver woven basket will always be in your garden for you, and it will be perpetually filled with these beautiful crystals. You can come to this part of your garden any time you feel the need, and you will always have access to the healing that comes from these glorious crystals of light and warmth . . .

The Value of the Self & Beliefs

The flowers are bending their heads towards each other and the many birds sitting on the trees' branches are twittering and preening themselves. The grass is cool beneath your feet and the trees are tall and in full leaf. The breeze gently ruffles their branches and moves lightly through your hair as you walk down your pathway to the fields. The trees are shaking their branches and the flowers are nodding their heads as though they are welcoming you as you pass by.

Can you smell the scent of the fields of flowers? Each flower has its own special aroma and together they blend into one cloud of fragrant perfume that wafts across the fields. The bees are humming as they busily fly from flower to flower collecting their pollen. The butterflies fly past in a rainbow of colour, the unusual markings on their wings showing the beauty of nature and creation.

You can walk through these fields, feeling the flowers touching you as you move through them. The flowers are very loving and caring, and they take great pleasure in showing their beauty and releasing their perfumes. You may care to lay down among the flowers, relishing the warmth of the sun on your body, as the flowers too enjoy its warmth on their petals. Bask in this warmth - and perhaps in the feeling of being a flower in all its beauty and glory - until you are ready to return to your pathway.

Noticing the small animals that you pass as you walk, you find that your pathway is taking you deeper and deeper into your garden, until you come to a small lake that sparkles and gleams in the sun's light. The grass is green and soft and feels like a cushion beneath your body as you sit by the water's edge. Weeping willows trail their branches like long fingers, as though to stir the waters. The lake gleams as it reflects the sunlight, while both white and black swans float serenely by. You can see small golden fish darting beneath the surface of the water. Your body absorbs the sun's warmth and you experience a sense of peace and serenity watching the calmness of the water and the beauty of the swans floating past.

Feel the freshness of the air surrounding you and breathe it in. Keep breathing it in and feel it cleansing your lungs, your body, your mind. You can feel the purification process that has commenced because of the freshness of this air reaching deep inside you. Allow this freshness to also reach deep within your mind and into your belief system, sweeping away the negative and restrictive thoughts and attitudes you have within you. Continue this until you feel as though you are now the air - clean, pure and perfect from this cleansing.

Because this freshness has entered and enlightened you, you will find that some of the values that have stayed with you for many years are changing. You may have grown up with values and ideas that are now cumbersome and no longer apply to you and your life.

Sit by the water and see each of your beliefs in front of you, supported by a pair of wings. Look at these beliefs and decide which ones you would like to retain and which ones you would like to let go.

Decide which beliefs you would like to keep, the ones you feel deeply and strongly about, and then have them move to one side. These may include beliefs that you are:

- good
- kind
- thoughtful
- sympathetic
- able to deal with problems in life
- able to give love to yourself
- able to give love to others
- that you have self-worth
- that you are worthy.

Look at the other beliefs - perhaps they are holding you back. Give considered thought as to why they no longer apply to you and your life - and then let them go. These beliefs may be:

- a lack of self-worth
- being an under–achiever
- an inability to love yourself
- an inability to love others
- being unable to cope on your own
- that you have no value
- perhaps even a feeling of being unlovable.

Let go of whatever beliefs constrain you. For each belief that you no longer want to retain, see the wings attached to them take them away from you, up into the air, and then vanishing. There is no need to keep anything that you do not believe in. You only need to retain those beliefs that support you, making you feel good about yourself, making you aware or making you feel comfortable within.

Allow your belief system to be open, to be flexible, to be your own. Know that you can be who you want to be just by being yourself, and be secure in your ability to love yourself and to love others also . . .

Your Spiritual Waterfall & Chakras

Feel the peace and tranquillity of your garden surrounding you as you enter it. The sky is an indigo blue and the clouds are small and scattered. The sun is a rich golden yellow and sends its light through the trees, gently dappling the flowers that are shaded by their branches. There are butterflies of many colours flying to greet you, landing softly on your shoulders and arms, some even settling on your hair. Their delicate wings create a kaleidoscope of colour as they weave their way towards you.

The sky is clear and the warmth of the sun radiates to where you are in your garden. The trees are whispering to each other and the mountains stand tall and graceful, outlined against the blue of the sky. The gardenia tree is full of blossoms, their whiteness contrasting beautifully with the rich shiny green leaves that appear almost to have been polished by a gentle hand. The perfume from these delicate flowers wafts towards you and you may care to take several of the gardenia tree's flowers with you as you wander through your garden.

Your pathway is taking you deeper into your garden and the butterflies fly before you, as though to show you the way. They are taking you to a magical part of your garden that you have not been to before. If you listen, you can hear the sound of water cascading, which has a musical quality. Follow this sound, and as you go around a bend on the pathway you will come towards a waterfall. The water is cascading down from the heights, sending droplets in all directions, each drop appearing like a gem being thrown high into the air as it catches and reflects the sun's light. This waterfall is a spiritual waterfall and has the ability to aid in your healing process by cleansing your chakras with its flowing waters.

Take yourself underneath your spiritual waterfall and allow yourself to be cleansed by this brilliantly clear, sparkling water. Feel the water falling around your body and lift your face up to feel its impact. The water sparkles in the sunlight, reflecting the sun's rays and making each drop appear like a perfect miniature crystal.

Feel the flow of the water slowing to a steady stream and allow it to enter through the top of your head. Take the water right through to your centre, so that it not only cleanses your outer body, but also the inner self.

Feel your concentration and thought-processes flowing, becoming fluid and clear as the stream of water enters and firstly cleanses your crown chakra. In doing so it awakens your consciousness, making you more aware of your spiritual self and your reason for being, before descending to each of your other chakras.

Feel this water flowing from your crown chakra to your third-eye or brow chakra, awakening your spiritual vision, thus enabling your inner vision to be clear and uncluttered, to see as you have never been able to see before. See the clarity this brings to your mind, which is then able to perceive the visions that are being brought to the surface of your sight.

Now take this flow of water to your throat chakra and feel how your throat is activated. Feel the energy pulsating there, and also feel that the words that will come from this centre will be pure and unselfish, with the ability to express with kindness and clarity.

This energy flow is now going from your throat chakra to your heart chakra, flooding the heart with its light. Droplets of water are entering each part of the heart, washing away any hurt or pain that may have been left from your past, or even from what you may be presently going through. Feel the love increasing within your heart chakra, enabling you to better love others and yourself, without selfishness. Also feel within yourself the expansion of compassion and understanding.

This steady stream is now ready to enter your solar plexus. It cleans this centre so that it is receptive and able to pick up energies from the environment, making you feel full and complete within.

From there, take the flow through to your spleen where it will remove unwanted toxins. This area is now strong, clear and pure, working capably and fully, and in line with the other chakras.

Now go to the root chakra at the base of your spine, taking through this crystal clear water. The water not only cleanses this chakra, but enables you to feel more earthed than you have been before, and more connected at every level of existence.

Because your chakras have now been cleansed by these spiritual waters you can feel how whole you are within yourself, and how every part of you now works in conjunction with each other. Stay as long as you want under your spiritual waterfall, and continue to feel the healing water flowing around you and in you. See the waters flushing out unwanted impurities and see them moving away from you. Know that the healing has commenced and will continue in the time to come . . .

The Large Rock & its Many Caves

As you enter your special garden the sun is sending out gentle rays that touch your body and make you feel especially good. Look around at the flowers that surround you and you will see that there are many bluebells raising their heads in the midst of the yellow daisies that are nodding in the gentle breeze. The lilies are scattered among them, their beautiful white faces and yellow tongues facing up to the sun's light, their snowy whiteness complementing the blue and yellow flowers that surround them. The sky is a crystalline blue and a few small clouds are carried across its surface by the gentle breeze, changing shape as they do so.

The air is fresh and clear and enters your body and lungs, clearing out the old, stale air to make way for the new air, giving you an added sense of vitality. Feel this air entering and take it right to the bottom of your lungs, cleansing and renewing as you breathe in this marvellous life force.

In the distance you will notice a large rock standing in relief against the skyline. The light from the sun makes the rock appear golden and seems to penetrate through it, taking away any darkness that may exist there. Go forward along your pathway, feeling the warmth of the earth beneath your feet. The trees are standing like sentinels on either side, their leaves moving slightly in the gentle breeze.

As you come closer to the rock, you see that it is even larger than you first thought. And now that you are facing it, you can notice that it has an uneven surface that gives the appearance of being rough. However some parts appear as if they have been polished and gleam where the sun's light falls upon them. From where you are standing, you can see there are many caves in this large rock and you may wish to enter some of them. Some of the caves are easy to enter as they are at the base of the large rock, while others have been formed by the wind and nature at a higher level. You may care to enter one of the higher caves for the moment, knowing that you can enter the others at any time you desire. The pathway is easy to climb, and there are colourful flowers growing in the crevices of the rocks and some small animals have come to watch you approach the series of caves.

On this occasion you may find yourself attracted to many caves, or perhaps only one. If you find yourself drawn to one particular cave then enter it. If a number of the caves attract you then, for your first excursion, choose the one that appears to be the best lit. Each of these caves represents a part of yourself that has not been acknowledged for a long period of time, and perhaps now is the right time for you to go within them in order to better understand yourself.

You will notice that the light that turned the rock golden has entered each cave, so everything is clear to you in the cave of your choice. You can go into any cave knowing that you are safe and secure in doing so.

There are many caves that you can enter that will reflect images of what you have accomplished or achieved. Look at your achievements and have pride in what you have done. The seeds have been sown and planted that will enable you to achieve your goals.

You may also see images from your past that you need to acknowledge and let go. There is nothing you cannot look at once you have acknowledged that those experiences belong in the past. Become the observer, not the participant. Allow yourself to simply observe everything and to feel the changes that happen when you do so, without participation. Feel the healing process commencing, alleviating the pain and hurt that have accumulated from these past experiences, and acknowledging the strength and purpose of your being.

You can always come to these caves in your special garden, and go within any of them to experience what is necessary to bring healing into your life. Life has so many experiences, so many events, that many may be beyond recall except in the subconscious. These caves will enable you to look within, to let go of what needs to be released and to rejoice over what has brought you happiness.

Have no fear. Have courage, because here you are free to be courageous. Acknowledge this and know that fear belongs in the past and courage will lead you into the future . . .

The Pool, The Lights & The Dolphins

The sky above your garden is filled with ballooning clouds that keep changing as the breeze encourages them to drift and to form different patterns against its brilliant blue. The sun hangs heavy above, highlighting everything around you with its golden light. You can feel its warmth touching your skin and gently entering your body, making you feel good inside.

There are butterflies of different species landing on the bushes and on the many fragrant flowers that abound in your garden. Their wings are fine and beautifully coloured. Some have a much larger wing span than others, which enables them to fly more quickly towards the tree or bush they have chosen. Their beautifully patterned and coloured wings create the impression of a moving rainbow as they fly from one part of the garden to another.

Follow these butterflies as they fly in front of you, creating a kaleidoscope of moving colour. They weave and turn before you, the gentle sun falling lightly on their wings, illuminating them, bringing their colour to life.

Your pathway will lead you to a large building that has slightly rounded sides, has no joins or sharp edges and is made entirely of glass. This building sits above steps that surround it on all sides, so that it appears to gravitate towards the heavens above. The building reflects the colours of the sky and the clouds, and indeed the garden itself appears to flow into its glass edifice. The richness of the garden's many flowers and other plants are being reflected, making the building appear as though it has been brushed by nature, thus creating a picture that could not be made by human hands.

Feel yourself climbing these stairs, going higher and higher towards the blue sky, until you reach the building's imposing entrance. High on the portals various signs and symbols stand in relief against the clearness of the glass. You may feel that these signs and symbols have special meanings that you can interpret. The healing energy contained in this building enters your body as you cross its threshold.

Deep inside this beautiful glass edifice, you come to a large pool. There are many coloured lights surrounding the pool, which is there for your healing. Why don't you enter these waters. They are warm, and you feel their buoyancy and healing qualities as you step into the pool. Feel the water washing over you, penetrating to the core of your being. You notice that the coloured lights surrounding the pool reflect the appropriate colour into the water, in order for your healing to commence. These lights keep changing and altering the colour of the water as the need within you changes and flows.

Allow yourself to float on these waters that are so buoyant. Feel the pain or the stress leaving your body, your mind, your soul, and feel the peace that is gathering in their place. Become aware that you are absorbing the colours from this magical water into yourself, and feel the difference these colours are making as the healing continues within you.

The far end of the pool narrows slightly, leading out into the ocean. Listen and you will hear a series of splashes from where the dolphins have entered. These dolphins are coming towards you and swim lazily around you, protectively. When you feel your energies are strong enough, perhaps you may care to swim with them. These dolphins will help in releasing any emotions that have been pent up inside you for too long. Perhaps you have kept your emotions hidden and have been unaware of their depth until now.

The dolphins will stay with you for as long as necessary. They will glide through the water with you, turning over lazily and with ease within these calm waters. Perhaps you may want to roll over as well, allowing the water to support and hold you safely and securely. You may like to play with the dolphins and to feel your laughter bubbling up as never before. Feel the joy of being with these magnificent creatures.

When you feel you have received enough healing from these calming waters, you may care to leave this beautiful building of glass, gliding with the dolphins through the far end of the pool, which enters into the depths of the sea. If you do so, you will find a similar feeling of peace and serenity there. You will feel more able and secure within yourself to experience the depths of the water, knowing that the dolphins will stay with you until you are ready to glide through the waters on your own...

The Golden Bell

There are birds of all descriptions calling to each other as you enter your garden, making a wonderful range of musical sounds that blend beautifully together, creating a sense of harmony and peace. They fill the branches of the many trees that grow within your garden, and these branches cast a protective shade onto the smaller plants that grow nearby, encouraging their growth.

The perfume from the flowers drifts easily throughout the other plants and trees. The flowers in their many colours move lightly with the breeze that stirs them, bending as though in tune to music that only they can hear.

The blue of the sky is light and delicate, and wisps of clouds drift slowly across its surface, sometimes leaving trails of white to linger in the sun's light.

The earth is soft beneath your feet and you can feel the peace and serenity that pervades your garden surrounding you. As you drift along your pathway, you will come to a small section of your garden that appears to be magical. It is filled with flowers and birds and butterflies. A myriad of colourful flowers cascades through the small plants and bushes, climbing up the trunk of some of the leafy green trees that stretch welcoming arms across them, shading the delightful flowers. Everything flows together with colour and light. The crystal-clear water from the small ornamental waterfall falls over smooth rocks, and tiny white flowers have formed around where it splashes onto the nearby earth.

Look around and you will see a large golden bell hanging suspended in the air. It is not held by anything that is visible to the eye and seems to move slightly in the gentle breeze. The sun's light brightens and illuminates this golden bell. Flashes of light dance from it onto the green leaves of the bushes and trees, and enriches the colour of the many flowers that flourish in the sun's light. This magnificent bell has fine etchings on its surface. These intricate patterns change according to how you feel and the nature of your illness. The etchings are symbols that relate to various parts of the body, and the one that is most predominant will correspond closely to the part of your body that is most in need at this time.

Underneath this bell is a cloth made of fine material unlike anything you have felt before. The cloth itself is impregnated with healing energies and it will aid in the healing you will receive from the golden bell. Lay down upon this cloth - which is soft and soothing to the skin - and you will feel the energy from it entering your body, making you feel comfortable and at ease. You can feel its warmth and gentleness penetrating your body and your inner self, breaking down any residual matter that is causing problems within you, thus bringing wholeness to your person.

Feel the power of the healing energies coming from this cloth, and feel yourself being permeated by them as you absorb this delicate yet strong energy.

The cloth beneath your body is raising you off the ground, so that you are suspended underneath the bell. Look up into the interior of the golden bell and you will notice that the clapper, or tongue, has been removed. This is the bell of peace and harmony and healing. Feel the gentleness of the light that emanates from this beautiful bell falling around your body, comforting it, easing it and uplifting it into its light.

The light from this glorious bell is falling completely around your body, surrounding you with its gentleness and healing power. This perfect light will be absorbed into your mind, removing negativity and fear, and filling you with the sensations of peace and tranquillity. It will enter through every pore of your body, bringing your body into perfect alignment with your spiritual and emotional aspects, enabling your mind and body to now work as one. This powerful and glorious healing light will help in maintaining the union of your body, mind and spirit.

Feel this perfect light penetrating your body, bringing healing to the parts of the body that are in need. Your healing bell sways gently over your body as the energies descend, permeating your body and your mind, enabling peace and serenity to enter. These healing rays entering you bring with them feelings of health and happiness that you may not have experienced for some time.

Feel yourself absorbing this healing energy into your body and into your mind, taking as much as is necessary for the moment, knowing that you can always return to this magical part of your garden and your beautiful golden healing bell at any time . . .

Becoming One With Everything in The Universe

A light breeze is drifting through the branches of the Grandfather Tree, and the rustle of his green leaves sounds like music. Flowers of various colours are thrusting their heads towards the light, seeking the warmth that will aid their growth. Some of the smaller flowers cluster together in the shade of the trees, and the light dapples through their leaves, touching each of them lovingly. As you go down your winding pathway towards a clearing, you feel the freshness of the grass and the dew beneath your feet.

The sky is a rich sapphire blue, hung with the merest wisps of cloud, and its richness is reflected in the waters nearby. The sun hangs like a giant golden globe, sending its warmth down onto the earth, enabling growth and life to be maintained.

Why don't you sit in the centre of the clearing, surrounded by the trees and bushes and watch the many animals stretching themselves as the sun's light surrounds them. The sun's warmth enters their fur, warming their muscles, and goes deeper into the innermost recesses of their bodies. The birds are gathering, the light breeze ruffling their feathers as they come in to land on the limbs of the many trees surrounding you.

Look at the insects that collect on the branches of these trees. The ants are busy as always, working together and helping one another take food to their loved ones. The caterpillars are slowly making their way through the trees' foliage, moving their many legs in unison.

Stretch your arms up towards the heavens and feel the vastness of the Universe surrounding you. Feel yourself being absorbed into your surroundings and feel your perceptions changing. Feel as though you and your surroundings are now as one. Experience yourself becoming one:

- with the seas, the lakes, and the waters,
- with the mountains and the hills,
- with the animals,
- with all plant life,
- with each stone,
- with the birds,
- with the earth,
- with the sun,
- with the sky,
- with the moon,
- with the stars,
- with the other planets,
- with the solar system,
- with the Universe,
- and becoming one with each and every person who lives.

Feel yourself breathing the fresh air, taking its cleanness deep into yourself. Feel it strengthening your lungs and aligning your inner person. Stretch your arms out wide, as though to embrace the earth and the whole Universe, and allow your voice to be heard. Hear your voice echoing out, touching everything that exists, vibrating through the trees and touching the skies.

Feel the earth beneath your feet, and notice its texture and warmth. Look at the majesty of the mountains and of your surroundings and be at one with them. Feel their peace and serenity reaching deep within you, touching you, and accept yourself as being the truth, as being strong, as being one.

- Become the mountain, strong and firm, reaching ever upwards towards the sky, sometimes capturing clouds to form around your uppermost tip.
- Become the sky and reach all around the earth and out into the Universe.
- Become the stars that beam their light to all who live on the planets beneath them.
- Become the sun and feel its warmth beaming out from you, helping the growth of all who feel its light.
- Become the moon and feel the mystery that comes from its depths.
- Become the earth and feel the footprints of all who tread upon it.
- Become the oceans and be at one with all the sea creatures that are replenished by you.
- Become at one with yourself, with the Universe, with all creation - become one with all that is . . .

The Pyramid

You can feel the warmth of the sun caressing you, its gentle fingers falling around your body as you wander down your garden path. There is a feeling of peace and gentleness surrounding you and the soft breeze touches you, making you aware of its presence. There is always serenity within your garden and all who live there reside in peace and harmony. You can feel the tranquillity within yourself becoming stronger as you absorb the peacefulness that exists within this beautiful sanctuary of yours.

The animals and the birds always love to come forward to greet you. Perhaps you see one that has been with you in the past and you may care to have it accompany you as you go deeper within your garden. Or perhaps you might like to choose an animal that you would not normally have by your side to guide you along your pathway.

The flowers are standing tall and strong with the sunlight aiding their growth, and they send their beautiful perfume through the nearby trees and bushes. Multicoloured butterflies land on some of the branches, and the sun's light picks up and magnifies some of their colours, highlighting the various patterns on their exquisite wings.

Looking into the distance, you see a pyramid that is surrounded by pure white light. Even though you are not close to this pyramid, you can feel the energy that comes from it resonating deep within you. This energy almost seems like sound as it enters your own personal space, surrounding you, encouraging you to take steps towards its source. Allow yourself to go towards the pyramid, feeling the evenness of your steps and your breathing until you find yourself before it. As you near its doorway, you will notice that the pyramid is much higher than it first appeared from the distance, its peak reaching as though to touch the sun, the sky and the clouds.

The entrance of the pyramid is tall and imposing, and as you enter you find that the inside of the pyramid glows with an incandescent light. This light appears to be funnelled through from its apex and then dispersed throughout the entire pyramid, filling it with light. The huge stone blocks glow and pulsate as the light that has gathered within each stone reaches out, giving warmth and comfort. Raise your arms and stand in the centre of this enormous pyramid, your head thrown back to receive this light. Feel the light falling completely around your body, encasing it with its healing properties.

There is a stone bed in the centre of the pyramid, directly below its peak. Lay down on this bed and you will find your body appears to sink into the stone with ease and comfort, as though the stone has been fashioned to support you. You can feel the warmth from the stone entering your body, warming it as it has never been warmed before, and the light from above is touching each part of your body with its energy force.

See this light penetrating your skeletal structure and feel its warmth entering your spine, touching each vertebrae, strengthening and realigning the spine so that it is lengthened and removing any calcification that may be there. You can feel your body softening, becoming fluid as the warmth becomes entirely absorbed throughout your body. This energy is travelling along your muscles, tightening and stretching them, but allowing them also to be flexible and free.

The light entering from the apex of the pyramid is streaming down upon you. The purity of this light is entering every pore of your body, making you feel good about the intensity of its light and its healing properties. Feel this beautiful stream of energy touching and healing every part of your inner body, which will then be reflected back as outer health.

Every organ of your body is receptive to this light and responds positively to its influence. Feel the strength of your heartbeat and the great capacity of your lungs to take in air. Feel your lungs being illuminated and filled with this light and energy. Allow this light to enter all parts of your body, and take it through your kidneys, gall bladder, liver, pancreas and spleen, as well as into the stomach and its lining. See the digestive tract as being able to absorb the healing properties this light brings, and to work in conjunction with each part of the body.

Stay there with these healing energies, which are being directed into your body from the light streaming from above, and also from the warmth and comfort coming from the stone bed you lay on.

Feel the healing being poured into you from this glorious golden light and inner warmth, and feel your body, your mind, your spirit, responding with health and vitality at all levels of existence . . .

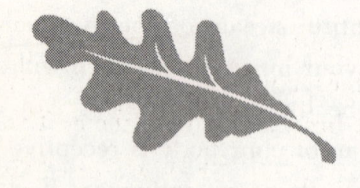

Cleansing Your Chakras With Colour

*I*n your garden the leaves on the spreading branches of the huge trees hang heavy, and yet they appear to dance with the light breeze that stirs them. The butterflies have come in all their wondrous colours, moving in the sunshine that dapples through the trees. Some butterflies have wings that are a rich blue and very large, with a lighter blue complementing and enriching the darker blue, thus making an intricate pattern. Other butterflies are small and pure white, except for their black eyes and feelers. Still others are orange with black tracings on their wings. And there are many more butterflies of different colours and patterns that glow as they move in the sunshine.

The sky is bright and clear, and its colour is a rich indigo blue. The light from this sky is like a cloak around you and the huge golden sun beams its liquid warmth towards you, touching you and making you feel good inside. You feel at peace within as these fingers of warmth fall around your body, helping to align your spine and bringing light and warmth into your mind.

The pathway in front of you winds its way in and out of the trees, and you feel safe and secure as you move your feet along its surface. The softness of the earth enters the soles of your feet, and you feel a spring in your step you have not felt for some time.

You may want to pick some flowers as you go further into your garden. You could make a small posy and carry it with you. If you do so, you will find other flowers appear in their place when you pick them, as nothing ever dies in your special garden. You can pick as many flowers as you want of various types and colours, and you will notice that the rose thorns will not prick your fingers because the thorns disappear as soon as the roses are picked.

Surround yourself with flowers of all colours and descriptions, the richness of their perfumes flooding your senses. The colour from the flowers is entering your body and connecting with your chakras. The colour from these flowers will cleanse them, enabling the healing to begin. Feel your chakras expanding as they experience the wealth of beauty and colour being directed towards them from these floral tributes, and also experience the cleansing these colours bring as they take life and energy into you.

Some of these flowers are becoming larger and larger, until seven of them are standing in front of you at various heights and with a slight space between them, so that each of the flowers is now aligned with one of your chakras. The light the flowers are sending into your seven chakras will aid in aligning and focusing them, so that your chakras glow with health, vitality and life as they absorb the colours.

Your seven main chakras are now standing out in relief from your body, absorbing the colours that are being reflected to you from the magnificent flowers that stand before you. As you absorb these colours, you will notice that each chakra takes on a different appearance and glows with the freshness of the colours taken into them. There is now a brightness within each chakra that was not there before, and as you allow this light to enter and to align each chakra you experience a lightness of being that you have not felt for some time.

Each of your chakras vibrates to a colour that is special to it, but sometimes you may feel the need to use other colours. You will attract the colours that are necessary for each chakra, depending upon what you need at this time, or perhaps you will make an adjustment or choice at the internal, intuitive level. Your body will call forth whatever colour is needed to make each chakra glow with health and vitality.

Each of your chakras now has a corresponding flower with the correct colour sending its light and energy forward towards you. These streams of light will enable your body to receive the right quantity and colour, not only to clean and clear your chakras, but to bring them into alignment.

Feel health and vitality entering you as these flowers send their healing energy into your chakras, making you feel more alive, more resilient, more receptive, more positive than you have been for some time. Feel this energy surging through you and feel the awareness this brings to your body, making you more aware than you have been before of the importance of the alignment of the spirit with the mind and the body . . .

The Rays of Light

You see how beautiful your garden is as you enter it. The flowers stand tall and still, and there is a sense of serenity and peace within, an air of stillness, of quietude. There are several small birds in flight, dipping and weaving in front of you, as though they want you to follow them. Feel the softness of the earth beneath your feet and breathe in the freshness of the air as you go forward.

You will notice rays of light shining through the trees as you go down your pathway, lighting it as though to show you the way. Some of these rays or beams will look brighter to you than others. These rays of light are the ones you should stand beneath, in order to feel their energy, their light, their love, their message, and to experience the healing that will be given to the area of your life or the part of the self that is in need.

There are many beams of light and each one of them has something different to give to you. Some represent:

- happiness
- joy
- the ability to give and to receive
- feeling complete within the self
- healing the hurt that exists
- lightening the heavy load you may have been carrying
- showing your spiritual self

- your childhood
- relationships
- self-esteem
- love
- peace
- tranquillity
- identification with the child within.

Other rays of light will represent whatever it is you need in your life at this point in time, knowing that time changes, allowing you to grow, to develop, to be as one, and to be at peace within yourself.

Walk into the first beam and you will find that it is filled with love. Allow yourself to absorb the love that is being given to you, taking it deep inside so that it can nourish your inner self. Allow this light to enter and lighten your heart, taking away any pain that may exist within. Feel the love surrounding you, replenishing you, thus enabling you to be a loving person who gives and receives love at all levels.

Go into another beam and feel yourself experiencing tranquillity. As you enter this ray of light you will feel yourself changing, becoming peaceful and serene as the light enters the core of your being, changing it, and pouring through feelings of tranquillity and making you feel whole, at one, and at peace with yourself.

Because you have entered the rays of love and tranquillity, perhaps you may now feel you would like to enter the ray of childhood dreams. You see yourself as a child who looked to the future knowing that you would be able to conquer the world. Feel the anticipation you had as a child, knowing then that nothing could harm you. See the child within and love that child now as you did then. Nurture and cherish this small child of yours that still lives within, and allow the dreams to grow.

As you are now feeling stronger and more complete, you may feel you would like to enter the ray that will heal any hurt that exists within your heart or your mind. This ray will enable you to go back in time to see how this hurt was created and why you have not released it. It has strong healing properties and will help you to release the pain associated with some of your past experiences. You have grown from these experiences, but now is the time to allow their memory to fade and to leave the pain where it belongs - in the past.

You may now care to enter the ray of light that deals with relationships. This warm light will show you how to cleanse past relationships and bring joy and peace into current ones. Perhaps emotions from past relationships are still having a negative effect on your life. These emotions no longer need to be with you, as these relationships belong in the past. Release them, let them go out into the Universe and allow yourself to live in the now. Feel the happiness that current and future relationships can bring and allow your feelings to flow, knowing that you are, and will be, loved and cared for.

Perhaps now is the time to go into the ray that deals with your spiritual self. Feel the intensity of this beautiful light surrounding and enveloping you, showing you the self that stands separate from your physical self. Look at the light emanating from this other self of yours and feel peace and understanding entering your physical body, aligning your heart, your mind and your body with your spiritual self. Feel yourself as being one entity, one soul, always surrounded by love, peace and tranquillity.

Go into those rays of light that you feel you would like to experience, and feel yourself accepting their healing rays. These beams of light will make you feel whole, complete, at one with yourself and at peace with all that is.

You have stood within the rays of light that you needed to experience at this time. Remember that you can always return to your garden and stand beneath other rays - when you feel the time is right and depending upon your needs.

All the beams of light that have illuminated you on this occasion have come together and formed a base beneath your feet. Now their individual strands of light are forming a cone of light to surround you, to protect you. Feel yourself being lifted up into the atmosphere by this glorious cone of golden light, knowing that you are safe, secure, loved, wanted - and complete . . .

Conception

As you enter your garden you can smell the wonderful perfume the flowers are sending forth as their aroma drifts around you. The slight wind moves through your hair and the air is fresh and cool. White clouds silently float above and the sun's gentle warmth falls like a light mantle around you, while the fallen leaves from the trees create a soft carpet for you to walk on.

The flowers are in full bloom and their strong aroma floats towards you, making you feel as though you would like to pick some of them. They are growing abundantly in their assorted colours of pink, purple, white and yellow, which complement the green shrubs and trees that stand nearby, as if to protect them. Small patches of violets are interspersed between the shrubs, and baby's breath adds its pale freshness, enlivening the colour of the violets.

The sky is a rich, beautiful blue, and tiny puffs of clouds have been sent scudding across its surface by the gentle breeze. The soft green grass glistens with the dew that has been left by the early morning mist. Why don't you lie down, feeling the softness of the grass beneath you, and watch the clouds drifting across the beautiful blue sky. Allow your thoughts to drift as the clouds do, feeling comfort within yourself as your body relaxes into the velvet softness beneath it.

Become aware, as you lay there, that a beautiful golden cone of healing light has appeared just above your body. This magnificent cone is pulsating with different lights that will be directed for some time into the lower part of your body, enabling the reproductive organs to glow and respond with health and vitality. Feel at ease with each and every light, knowing that you can work with them and that you can feel their healing energies. Feel yourself relaxing further into the luxurious green grass, being supported by its softness and its strength.

There are rods of silver light entering your Fallopian tubes, cleansing them, purifying them. These small lights of energy are being taken through your tubes so that they are made clear. These rods will remove any unwanted obstacles, cleansing and purifying your tubes to enable conception to begin.

Your ovaries and womb are being bathed in a gentle blue light. Feel this light being absorbed into these parts, allowing the healing properties brought by this colour to enter. Your reproductive organs are vibrating with this light and you can feel the healing energy entering each organ, each tissue, bringing optimum health and vitality to each of them.

Now bring through a delicate green. See this green gradually being absorbed into each area and see each part of your reproductive system glowing with its light. Feel its light and warmth as it enters, bringing its own gentle healing properties. Green is a lovely regenerative colour that brings growth to each organ that is in need.

Take through the glorious colour of red, and feel its richness as it enters and replenishes the blood supply.

Feel it pulsate through your organs, enriching and revitalising each of them in preparation for pregnancy. See the surrounding tissue as being clear and healthy, with no problems obstructing the energy flow between your organs.

The wall of the womb may need to be strengthened. See a golden light forming as a mist and then entering the womb, becoming stronger as it penetrates the walls and strengthens them in order for the baby to be carried successfully. Concentrate on these walls and see their strength growing through the action of this glorious golden light, which makes them vital and energised.

As pink is the colour of love, now also take this colour through your womb in preparation for the child. Allow this pink to be all pervasive and to enter each and every part of the womb, saturating it with love, peace and vitality. Then the child, when conceived, will feel the love emanating from its place of growth, surrounding it always.

Now take through into each and every part of your body - into the heart, the lungs, the stomach, the spine, the other organs - all the colours that you feel are right for you. See your own beautiful rainbow filled with colours richer and deeper than you have ever seen before. Feel which colours are right for you and experience the joy, pleasure and warmth they bring. See all of the parts of your body resonating to each and every colour that has been taken through them, enabling your organs to be productive and to work at their optimum, and now allow these healing energies to enter not only your reproductive organs, but your entire body.

Feel the peace that these colours have brought with their healing properties, and know that the serenity that comes from this healing will stay with you in the time to come . . .

Your Unborn Child

Feel yourself walking along the pathway in your garden, the sun's gentle fingers falling across your body. It is sending its golden rays down, lighting up the branches on the trees and placing a glow around all that it touches. The sun's rays go deep into the earth, helping the grass and other plants to grow, and everything you see around you seems to glow with its light.

The flowers are pushing their heads forward to catch the sun's golden rays and are nodding as if to greet you as they send out their beautiful perfume. The air is fresh and ruffles your hair as if a hand is playing with it. The light breeze rustles through the leaves of the many trees that are in your garden.

The sunshine is lighting your garden in a special way. There are petals from many flowers strewn across the velvet green grass and their colours vibrate within the sun's light. They form a rich multicoloured carpet for you to lay on. Gently lay down upon this luxuriant bed of petals and allow yourself to feel their softness and to smell their perfume surrounding you, encompassing you, so that you feel especially good. Feel the light of the sun shining onto your body, making you feel warm, at ease and comforted by the light and energy coming from this star.

You may care to look back to the time prior to your own day of birth, when you existed within the womb and were carried everywhere comfortably. You may remember the feelings and sensations you experienced, the way you heard, the way you felt, and how you saw within your mind's eye. You were aware of conversations, of music, of sound, of feelings. Perhaps you were unwilling to depart from this place of peace and security, but you could feel the love directed to you from those who were gathering around as they waited for your moment of birth.

Now you are at a precious time in your life when you yourself are carrying a small one within your womb. This small life is absorbing nutrients from your body and is being carried very carefully.

Send love to your own unborn child, the one you are carrying so close to your heart, the one who is growing beautifully within your womb. This precious soul has been brought to you for you to nurture, to care for, to love, to bring to life. Talk to this glorious child who is being carried within you. Sing to the babe within you and play music to calm and soothe this small one who is soon to leave its place of comfort. Picture yourself holding this long-awaited one when the moment of birth comes, and your babe will also be able to share this experience, thus sensing the joy this birth will bring for both of you.

Feel this new life within yourself, feel the stirring that this small babe has brought, and you will find your heart opening with love and joy, and you will experience bliss. This tiny parcel of happiness has chosen you as its birth mother, having looked down from the heavens to decide who the parents would be. With love and thought, you have been selected to carry and care for this child, and all caring commences in the womb.

Feel yourself communicating with the small one within your body. And hear the communication being returned. Speak to the babe who is growing within you and see your partner also communicating with both of you, expressing love and happiness.

See a golden light entering your body, touching every part of your inner self. See it entering your tubes, your ovaries, your womb, touching and enlivening the small parcel of happiness that you carry. Feel the peace and serenity that this light brings, and experience the love being returned to you. Know that you are united as one . . .

The Stars & the Miniature Waterfall

The trees in your garden are looking especially beautiful in the moonlight. Their branches are gently moving the moon's light through their greenery until its pearly fingers touch the ground. The light breeze is drifting through the branches, rustling their green leaves, and the sound is like music.

Your garden is very quiet and still, and the flowers have tilted their heads back to be bathed in the light from the many stars above. This light streams down, mingling with the light from the full moon that also hangs in the sky. The moon's rich, incandescent light bathes you, moving you to feel its full beauty. Your garden is quiet, so quiet you believe you can hear the grass and the flowers growing. Some of the flowers and bushes have been highlighted by the golden glow that pulsates from the orbs of beauty above.

The moon's light is pouring down on the nearby grass as though it were impregnating the earth with its light and energy. Why don't you lie down upon this bed of light to look at the many stars above you and the patterns they have formed. There are some stars that appear larger and brighter than others because they are bigger or closer to the earth, while others twinkle more dimly from far, far away. Some stars form the pattern of a pathway, as though they have traffic passing through them, while others stand alone on a solitary path.

The Universe is wide and deep and holds an abundance of yet to be solved mysteries. There are many planets within this Universe, many of which are undiscovered. The moon's light mingles with that of the stars and brightens the way for all travellers in time, enabling you to go far beyond this earthly realm.

You can hear the sound of water falling as though from a height, and you now see before you a stream of running water that is crystal clear. The moon is catching the reflection of its own light within the water that cascades over the rocks from a miniature waterfall, which enables you to see clearly into these waters. The reflection in these waters of the night sky - with its beautiful full moon and its myriad of stars - is so clear that you feel that you could actually touch the images you see within the waters. Perhaps you may like to put your hand into the cool waters to see if you can catch any of the images in your hand.

Sitting in the middle of the stream is a rock that has been pitted by time and the elements. Why don't you allow the waters to take you to the aged rock. There you can feel the light from the stars and the moon streaming around you and enveloping you. As you sit upon the rock you find that it brings you comfort, and you can feel its age and wisdom permeating your body. Perhaps you can now experience how it feels to be this aged rock that has stood the test of time, that has experienced the water lapping around it for centuries, with either the sun beaming its light down upon it or with the light from the moon surrounding it. As you listen to the gently moving waters, feel the peace and serenity that surrounds you and the quietness of your garden will revive your spirit.

When you are ready, lay down in these refreshing waters and allow them to flow around your body. Feel the waters refreshing, renewing and enlivening your spiritual self. The waters are buoyant and carry your body with their motion, rocking you gently from side to side so that you feel contentment at a deep level and whole within yourself.

Lay there, feeling comforted and protected by the motion of the water, with the light from the moon and the stars gently beaming down to where you are. Feel these lights entering your being, and gently allow them to connect with your inner self.

You feel at ease as you become aware that your emotional self is being supported by these delicate lights as they enter you and connect with your heart. It is as though these lights are now flowing from your mind to your heart, so that the feelings from these areas can easily flow from one to the other, with love and understanding.

Feel these gentle lights touching your emotional self so that you feel it is aligned with everything within the Universe. Know that all is well within your inner world . . .

Your Soul, Your Spirit

The light blue sky is cloudless and reflects the sun's rays into your garden, bringing its light and warmth around you. The butterflies in their many beautiful colours fly before you, and some will land upon your hair and your shoulders, bringing delight as they do so. The sunlight dappling through the tall trees touches the delicate wings of those butterflies who fly in front of you, leading you deeper and deeper into your garden.

The trees seem to be whispering as the gentle breeze moves their branches and foliage, and the songs of the many birds that have built their nests within the comfort of these trees fill the air. Now the nature spirits who live within your garden are showing themselves to you. They will show you how they care for the trees that grow to be tall and majestic, how they nurture the flowers that impart their glorious perfumes while bringing the beauty and colour of their petals into view, and how they look after the smaller bushes, trees and other plants. These gentle and shy nature spirits adapt to the colour of the particular plant they care for, which is why we are sometimes unable see them.

You can feel the warmth of the sun caressing you as you walk within your garden, and the gentle breeze moves around your body, touching it lightly and moving through your hair with light fingers. You can hear the birds calling to one another and you feel the peace that exists within your garden. Here nothing can harm you - all who live within its sanctuary live in peace and harmony.

Feel this peace and harmony penetrating to the very core of your being, going deep inside you, touching those parts of your inner self that are in need of healing, and allow this healing to take place. See any disharmony that exists within your inner self melting away and being changed into a positive sense of harmony and health that is being returned into your being, allowing your inner person to feel as one and at peace within.

See your heart expanding, growing larger with love for yourself and for all those around you. Any pain that has existed because of disharmony within the self or with others is being taken away, leaving you with a greater sense of serenity and peacefulness of spirit than you have experienced for some time. You can feel the adjustment taking place within yourself as your spiritual body aligns itself with your physical, emotional and mental bodies, bringing with it contentment and peace.

Your eyes are being adjusted so that you can perceive yourself with your spiritual eyes, enabling you to see your soul or spirit standing in front of you. You can now see a soul who has great beauty within, whose light shines forth attracting others of like mind, and who feels contentment and peace within at the deepest level. The light that is emanating from this spiritual part of the self lights the area around you, illuminating and touching all that exists. Look at this light and see its purity as well as the intensity of its glow. Realise that this is the real you, and that the physical body is only the envelope or overcoat to house the spiritual self while you are here on this earth.

As you look at the beautiful light that beams forth from your spiritual self and touches all around, remember that this 'real you' is the one that is connected to the God Force, so that you are never alone. Experience not only the feelings of freedom that being this light brings, but also the sense of awareness you have of all that exists. Rejoice and know that your spirit, your soul, is aware of the difficulties you have encountered during your time on the earth plane. Feel love and strength coming from this part of the self towards you, making you feel whole and complete.

The spiritual part of the self is the self that has always existed, has always known all there is, and has been able with ease to tap into the collective unconscious for healing at any level. Allow your spiritual self to go into the collective unconscious in order for healing to take place, and know that your inner beauty and light will bring to you at this time that which is necessary for wholeness of your inner self. Know that you are not only a physical being but a spiritual one, and that your spiritual light glows and attracts to you those of like mind . . .

Healing With Colour

You can feel the peace and serenity of your garden flowing around you and into you. The trees stand tall and steadfast, their leaves full of life. They appear to be reaching for the white ballooning clouds that are drifting slowly across the radiant blue sky, as though to pull them around the very tips of their branches. The brilliant golden sun beams down, revealing the gloss of the leaves and the rich depth of their green. Many small insects crawl along the branches, luxuriating in the sun's warmth that also nurtures the tiny new leaves that are just beginning to form there.

You can see that the flowers are thriving in the sun's light, and how their many colours enrich and enliven the brown earth. The roots of the trees and bushes reach deep within the earth's surface, seeking nourishment.

And now look up from the earth, to the heavens above. Feel yourself going beyond our world as we know it and see the Universe, which is wide and deep and mysterious. See not only the sun, the moon, the other planets and the stars, but go beyond what is known, seeing distant galaxies and stars being born. Feel the vastness of the Universe, and know that it is full of purpose and spirit. As you float in the midst of the cosmos, now see the Universe as being filled with brilliant white light that streams towards you, bringing consciousness, awareness and understanding. This glorious light brings also a depth of feeling and peace that you can take inside and store within your soul, your spirit, your body, your very being. Take this white light entirely through yourself, noticing how it enlivens and enriches your body and brings peace and happiness to your inner self. Feel the light's strength as it enters and touches each organ, each vessel, each tissue, and feel it coursing through your blood supply, stimulating and activating each part of the body it touches.

Now you find that you have returned to your special garden and you have become aware that deep within you a new understanding of your oneness with the Universe is blossoming. You feel as though that you are becoming one with the earth, its trees, bushes, flowers and water, becoming one with the sky, the clouds, the sun, the moon, and indeed the endless Universe beyond. You feel in tune with all that nature and the Universe has to offer, and that they are now offering you their colours for your healing. The colours that enter your body will help to bring your entire being into alignment, so that your spiritual, mental, emotional and physical bodies work as one.

Bring down the golden light from the sun, feeling its warmth and energy caressing you, infiltrating your system through the pores of your skin and entering your entire body. Take this golden light slowly through your body, letting it touch and enliven each part, and then feel life stirring within all levels of your being, bringing awareness and peace.

Feel the blue of the sky reaching down and touching you, entering you. See its brilliance being absorbed into each part of your body, bringing health and vitality to those organs in need and creating a feeling of tranquillity within your soul.

Absorb the green from the bushes and trees that always stand as sentinels for you when you enter your special place, your special garden. Allow its healing properties to be absorbed, to be taken to the place in the body where they can do the most good. See this colour of regeneration helping to rejuvenate those areas of your body that are in need, and see the colour and health of each of these being restored.

Take the yellow from the daffodils and allow it to enter your mind. See this glorious, rich colour entering any negative dark spots, enlightening or removing them, enabling your beautiful mind to be clear, focused and unencumbered, and removing all doubts, uncertainties and fears. See your mind working at its optimum, with clarity and foresight, and see ideas and thoughts flowing freely as an expression of your individuality.

Standing before you is a magnificent rose in the fullest of its bloom. Accept the pink from this rose and allow its rich colour to reach deep within your heart. Absorb its beauty and feel your heart flourishing like the rose in its fullness and beauty and know that your heart will become kinder and softer for having used this beautiful colour. See this pink entering each chamber of your heart, cleansing it, removing any impurities and taking away any hurt or pain that may exist there. Your heart is left feeling full and complete, with a deeper love for yourself, as well as for others.

Now see a beautiful red tulip before you, and take the depth of its colour through your bloodstream. See the richness of this red removing toxins and unwanted waste from your body as it enlivens your blood supply, your veins and your arteries, enriching them so that your entire being sparkles with health and vitality. Feel your energy supply coming to its optimum, along with a need to be up and doing, with energy to spare.

In front of you there are rich purple violets, whose depth of colour you want within you. This glorious purple - the highest of the spiritual colours - is being totally absorbed into your being, enlivening, enriching and encouraging growth at all levels of your many different bodies, your many different selves. See your spiritual understanding and sensitivity increasing as this colour goes deeply within you, and feel the compassionate part of your nature coming more to the fore. Feel this magnificent colour forming a cloak that surrounds you, enabling all the healing colours to work within every level of your being during the days, the weeks, the months to come . . .

The River Of Life &
The Rainbow

As you enter your garden, the many flowers that reach for the sun's rays send their fragrance towards and around you, as though to welcome you on your special journey. The sun is high in the heavens and sends its gentle warmth to where you are, surrounding you and your pathway with its light. The blue of the sky is light and delicate, and small wisps of white cloud float serenely by. The grass is cool beneath your feet and the trees are tall and in full leaf as they reach towards the sky, casting shadows to protect the small plants that grow nearby. The breeze gently sways their branches and moves lightly around you as you walk through your garden.

The freshness of the air surrounds your body, caressing your cheeks and ruffling your hair. Breathe this cool, clear air into your lungs and feel it cleansing and replenishing you as it enters deeply within your body, removing the old and stale air that has resided there for so long.

Feel the peace and tranquillity that flows through your garden and the gentleness that exists there. Your path is winding through the trees and takes you to a beautiful lake surrounded by weeping willows, whose long fingers dangle in the water and move to and fro with the water's motion.

There is a simple wooden boat moored there, with a small canopy at one end for shade. The inside of the boat is lined with rich, colourful fabric. As you step inside the boat and lay upon the fabric, you feel its silkiness against your skin. This small craft is going to take you along the calm waters of the River of Life. The River of Life enables you to look at past experiences and bring to the fore the feelings associated with those experiences, and then to let them go. You will be shown only those experiences that you can deal with at this moment in time.

Relax into your boat, feeling the softness yet supportiveness of the fabric beneath you, knowing that you do not have to steer this craft. As it makes its own way down the River of Life, the sun's light falls around you with a soothing warmth and the sensation of the gentle waters beneath the boat brings comfort.

Your boat will take you along your River of Life, showing you experiences that may have been sad or happy; times when you have been thoughtful of yourself, or foolish in that regard; feelings you have had when you have been alone, or when you have been surrounded by friends. You will see many experiences that you have forgotten, but which have been buried in the recesses of your mind. Now you can see them, but without feeling the intensity of the emotions they aroused at the time of their occurrence. Look at them - and let them go.

As you drift along the waters you may see some of the milestones that you have experienced in your life. You have the ability to see and understand why these things have occurred in your past, but without now experiencing the fear and hurt that may have come with these experiences. Look at them - and let them go. Know that they belong in the past and no longer have relevance for where you are in your life now.

Other experiences will come forward as you go further along your personal river and you may look at these with joy and happiness, re-experiencing the feelings that came with them at the time of their happening. Look at them - and let them go. Know that you will have many more experiences that will bring you joy and happiness.

Feel the joy the sun's light is bringing to you as you luxuriate in its warmth while calmly drifting down the River of Life. Look ahead and you will see there is an enormous rainbow crossing over your beautiful waterway. The sun's rays gleam around and through it, bringing into relief the many hues of this special rainbow.

Your small wooden craft takes you directly under this glorious rainbow and stops there so that you can receive the rainbow's healing rays. Feel the colours from this rainbow being directed into your boat and feel the joy this brings into your body, into your being, into your inner self, into your soul. Some colours may be more intense than others. Accept this intensity, and then allow these colours to be modified and changed to suit the healing that is required for you.

When you have received the healing you require, your boat takes you beyond the rainbow and down your River of Life. You now see with new eyes and new feelings. You feel an inner strength surfacing that has always been there, but perhaps it is one that has been hidden or has not surfaced for a period of time. This inner strength flows through you, and you feel love and understanding, and a new sense of acceptance of yourself, as well as of others.

Be at peace, be at one with yourself, and know that your boat, your River of Life, and your rainbow are always there for you . . .

World Healing

*E*nter your inner garden, your sanctuary, and feel peace surrounding you, flooding through your body, your mind, your soul, your spirit, and know that you are one with the Universe. Look at the beautiful trees and flowers in all their glorious colours and luxuriate in their beauty. The sun's rays are being directed towards you and its warmth settles around you like a gentle cloak. The clear blue sky is as rich as a sapphire, and a few small clouds drift across its surface. Become aware of the earth beneath your feet, soft and warm, welcoming your footsteps as you go along your pathway.

You see water lilies drifting on a pond that is surrounded by trees whose reflections are mirrored within its depths. Sit by this calming water and feel stillness and healing energies gathering around you. Know that you are going to pass on these energies to those in need throughout the world.

There is a stream of beautiful white light coming around you as you sit. You feel connected with this spiritual light, knowing that you can send not only this pure light, but also light of various colours, out into the world for healing. Feel the intensity of this glorious light entering you, touching each part of you, until you feel that you are of the light itself and able to send this light out into the world for its healing.

Now see this glorious white light being sent by you as a mist, going high above your own special garden and being taken across the countryside, going over the land, the waterways, the homes, the institutions, the orphanages, the cities, being directed to all who are in need as the light makes its way and connects with all who require healing.

Direct this light across the oceans, see it touching the waters and the islands, and then being taken across the vast expanses of land as it reaches each country. This light is going to penetrate and be absorbed into the areas where it is needed, and it will be taken to the places where it can do the most good.

- Send healing lights to all those who are incarcerated or institutionalised, helping them to feel the comfort, peace and serenity of the spirit that may have been lacking within them for a long time.
- Take this powerful healing light into orphanages and see it touching each child gently. See them being comforted and uplifted into the light, easing the pain of their aloneness and aiding them in seeing a future that has hope.
- Take it into the hospitals and see it entering those who are ill, and see the intensity of this light healing at the very source of each illness.
- Take this glorious light into psychiatric hospitals and similar institutions, and see it bringing peace to the minds of those who reside there, stilling the torment that disrupts their mental processes and enabling clarity to enter their thought processes.

- Take it into the jails, in order that healing and understanding may be given to the inmates, so that they no longer feel the need for violence. Also send the healing lights to their victims so they can receive healing for the injustice and other harm that was done to them.
- Go with this glorious light into the countries where famine exists, and where children and adults die through neglect and lack of care. Also take this pure light through the countries where brother fights brother and disunity reigns, and see it being absorbed by them, enabling peace to be restored and love to reign.
- See peace, simplicity and love being felt within the inner part of the soul of each person in need.

And now you see a painter's palette in your hand, filled with colours that are richer and purer than any you have seen before. You are able to choose the colours that you feel are the most appropriate to be sent into the world for its healing at this time.

One by one, send each of the colours you select out into the world, seeing them drift away as mists and knowing that each will enter and touch all those who will allow these healing energies to surround them.

These mists will drift over the many lands and across the seas, the mountains, the islands and the deserts, and be taken into each part of the world where healing is required. See these colours bringing harmony and understanding into the lives of the many who are in need, and see all they touch being united as a positive force of energy, goodwill and love towards each other and their fellow man . . .

Earth Cleansing

Look around your beautiful garden and you will see silver raindrops glistening on the green leaves and the velvety grass. The flowers, in their many colours, move gently in the light breeze shaking some of the drops from their bodies, which fall to the ground as though to replenish it yet again. As you walk, the grass is soft beneath your feet and their imprints vanish as the grass springs back to its original fullness. The bees are flying from flower to flower, collecting the pollen and making small sounds that contribute to the feeling of the peace and serenity that exists within your special garden.

Feel the deep sense of care you have for the earth itself, its animals and small insects, its surrounding waters and the water birds and fish that abound therein, and for the air that you breathe and the birds that fly so effortlessly without tiring. Feel how interconnected every part of the earth is with its waters, its air and the life it brings forth - the birds and reptiles, the insects and mammals, the plants and fish, and the animals large and small. Sense the importance of them living together in harmony and peace. Look at the sun and its light, which brings warmth and growth to everything that lives, and marvel at this planet of ours in all its beauty and splendour.

Above you are huge, ballooning clouds that are filled with healing water. The land needs to be nourished so that the creatures who inhabit the earth can live and grow. The larger plants need to be nurtured so that they reach their lush maturity, so creating shade for the smaller ones. This healing water is now raining down very gently and touching each plant, each tree, each flower, and they are responding by opening themselves up totally to the beautiful fluid that is being freely given to them. The rich, nourishing fluid is penetrating the soil and the desert deeply. The colours of the flowers are intensifying, the green of the plants and trees becoming richer and deeper, and the soil and deserts are flourishing as never before.

You can see the water making tracks along the leaves and the petals, cleansing and purifying each of them before being absorbed into the stem or trunk. This healing water is then taken deep into the soil, enabling the growth of the trees, the flowers and the shrubs to be richer and more vibrant than before.

The earth itself is taking these waters deep down into its core, where some of this nurturing fluid will be retained and stored. This marvellous fluid will then replenish and nourish the small, new roots of plants that are now being encouraged to grow in areas that have had no growth for some time.

The seas, the rivers, lakes, tributaries and ponds are being showered with this healing fluid and their water levels will rise to heights that are correct for them. The impurities that they have had are being eradicated by the healing water that has been added to their depths. Fish of many colours are now able to be seen as the water is crystal clear. Many of these fish jump and leap out of the water with joy, before parting the water's surface to enter again beneath its benign veneer.

The rainforests, with all their unique, beautiful plants, are welcoming this shower of healing rain and are reaching out for nourishment. The native birds and animals that thrive in this environment show themselves in all their beauty as they too welcome this heavenly nectar.

The animals and the birds that exist everywhere are coming out to stand beneath these beautiful full clouds and their healing waters, and they are welcoming the feeling of this rain upon their coats and their feathers. They feel the water cleansing them, strengthening them, energising them. The nourishment from this water is being felt by even the smallest insect, and they revel in the healing properties of the water being directed to them.

The waters are continuing to come down on each part of the earth, to each animal, to each plant, to every part of nature, restoring each of them to their own individual wholeness and beauty. They appear to preen themselves as they absorb this healing water. It washes away any impurities that may exist, bringing new growth and vitality to all.

Observe the clouds above and you will now notice that they are becoming smaller and smaller now that the healing purity of their waters has penetrated each and every living part of the world and its earth. The clouds are changing their form and now float lazily in the sublime blue sky.

The sun's rays are coming through these clouds and its golden light is filtering down to the earth below with its many creatures and plants. This glorious light is bringing an upsurge of energy to all as its rays increase in intensity, until the sky and the earth are bathed in its warmth, encouraging new growth and life . . .

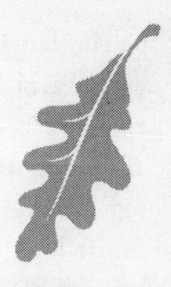

Grief & Loss

The sun hangs overhead like a rich golden globe, filled with warm light that bathes you in its delicate glow. The gentle breeze ruffles your hair as it moves through your garden, and the freshness of the air brushes your face lightly as though with fingers. The sky is a velvet blue and powdery clouds drift high above, making intricate patterns that are ever changing. The grass and the dew are cool beneath your feet and butterflies of many different colours crowd around the violets, lilies and daffodils that abound in profusion, their perfume drifting around you on the light breeze.

The Grandfather Tree has many birds nestling among his branches, some of them fluffing their feathers as they settle down to rest. Others are feeding their little ones in nests where they will be protected and secure until they are big enough to fend for themselves. This wise old tree rustles his green leaves and moves his heavily laden branches as though to welcome you.

His solid roots form large mounds that reach deep into the earth, creating seats comfortable enough to sit upon. Choose one that allows you to sit close to his thick trunk, beneath his sturdy branches that are heavy with rich green foliage, as the light breeze fans your face. Feel the strength of this wise old tree touching you, helping you deal with your feelings of pain and loss, helping to alleviate your grief or perhaps even feelings of guilt. You may be feeling guilt because you did not help loved ones who have passed on as fully as you would have liked. Or perhaps you feel guilt because you are the one left behind rather than your loved one.

You may feel your grief is too hard to bear and that you cannot share with others what you are going through. Put your arms around the trunk of this beautiful tree and allow your tears to freely flow. See your tears soak into the bark, going through the tree and then into the earth, as though to replenish and nourish it in order for new growth to appear.

See your tears leaving you, being absorbed into the tree and the earth, and then see small golden-green leaves shooting up among the older leaves. Notice how the sun's rays seek them out to encourage their growth.

Feel the glow of the sun surrounding you, its intensity lightening your burden with its rays of comfort. Take its warmth deep inside yourself, into your heart, into your soul, and see these rays being dispersed throughout your body, their light entering into all parts of you. Feel these rays slowly entering your heart, helping to alleviate and remove the pain that has been pulsating there. Feel your heart opening up, changing, and as your grieving changes, you will be able to let go of fears, doubts and uncertainties. As the compartments of your heart open, it will become more receptive and able to release grief, and you will be more able to allow other feelings and experiences to enter.

Your arms reach comfortably around the old tree's trunk. You begin to understand that you too can be like this tree, having strong foundations and being able to withstand whatever life has to offer. Knowing that you have the courage and vitality to go forward in life, you now feel more able to cope with the feelings of grief or loss that have been surrounding you.

Hold onto the trunk of this wise old tree and you may see some of your life experiences being replayed before you. You might see the sad times when you have felt your energy being dissipated by having too many problems thrust upon you, when you have lost loved ones, or when you have felt used or abused by those close to you. Other experiences may show difficulties and fears that you have had and which you overcame, and how you gained strength from learning how to deal with those problems.

You will also see many of the times when you felt complete, when you felt whole, when your energy was high and you felt the potency of life flowing through you. Look forward to what life has to offer and know that your energy is rising. Feel life flowing through your veins, your blood, drawing you away from pain and into the fullness of life. There are times coming when you will experience great joy, great happiness, when you will feel powerful and strong and in control of your own destiny.

Feel yourself coming to the realisation that life moves on and you must go forward into life, into living, into loving.

Allow your tears to flow for the moment, and know that time is fleeting, that change is coming, and that you will come out from this moment being more resilient, more able, with strong foundations and the ability to go forward in life . . .

Releasing Stress

Feel the peace flowing through your garden, touching you, entering your body, making you feel good inside. The air is fresh and clean, and as the gentle breeze flows around your body you feel it taking away any pain or discomfort that you may have. Listen and you will hear the sounds of birds singing, their beautiful voices reaching far into every part of your special garden.

The green grass is lush and stretches in front of you like an undulating carpet, inviting you to walk further within your garden. Listen to the sounds of the birds as you go along a pathway you have not experienced before, feeling the softness of the earth beneath your feet. Smell the aroma of the many flowers that are swaying in the breeze, releasing their perfume to drift among the trees and bushes.

A golden lion is coming towards you, shaking his beautiful mane in welcome. As he comes closer, place your hand upon his body, feeling the warmth and softness of his fur, the strength of his muscular body and the gentleness of his spirit. You can feel his strength entering your hand and going into your body, making you realise that strength is not only an outwardly physical attribute, but also an internal one, and that gentleness is strength of a different kind.

Keep your hand on the lion's mane and allow this magnificent creature to take you deeper and deeper within your garden, until you come to a large oak tree. This tree's branches reach towards the sun, the clouds and the sky, as though to embrace them, and its roots enter the earth deeply, causing mounds to erupt that are comfortable enough to sit upon.

Why don't you sit upon one of these mounds, leaning your back against the tree's trunk? Your golden lion is stretched out nearby, relaxing in the shade of the tree as the sun's light dapples through the branches and falls upon his fur.

The glorious oak tree has chosen to absorb any stress you have in your body, or in your mind, and will always be available for you at any time you are carrying undue stress or discomfort.

Feel your spine relaxing as you lean against the bark of this oak tree's trunk and feel each vertebrae being straightened as you do so. The strength of the tree enters your spine and absorbs any stress within your body. Feel it also absorbing any negativity in your thought processes that may be causing your spine to stiffen or become rigid. Your mind is all powerful, and the tree's energies will help your mind to expand as well as to release thoughts that may be restricting your progress.

Look into yourself and realise why you have allowed yourself to become stressed, why you have accepted the conditions that are now causing you pain. You do not have to accept these conditions any longer. Relax into the trunk of this beautiful tree - and let these conditions go. Whatever is causing you stress or discomfort within yourself - let it go.

Relax against the trunk of the tree and see the stress that has been stored within your body entering the bark and being pulled into the tree, relieving you of your tension and pain. See the stress that was in your body going up the tree's trunk as electrical impulses, entering its branches and leaves, and then being pulled like electrical sparks up into the atmosphere. You will notice that these electrical sparks, which are stress leaving your body, are now exploding into the sky, into the wind, into the clouds, causing a powerful storm to erupt. Hear the thunder, and look at the brilliant flashes of lightening that are now occurring high in the heavens above.

Open your arms wide and welcome the downpour of rain as it reaches you. Feel the beauty of this water cascading around you, washing through you, taking away any residue of mental, emotional or physical stress that may have been left behind. Feel the purity within yourself. Feel the clarity of mind this brings. Feel the difference it makes to your spirit, your body, your emotions. Feel how powerful the water is as it washes away any feelings of guilt or remorse, of not being good enough, of not being understood, and then feel how powerful you have become within.

Now that the tree has absorbed the stress and the waters have washed away any residue that may have remained, stand up and open your arms wide to the Universe. Welcome nature to gather around you in all her awesome wonder, with all her beauty and strength.

And now feel the gentle rays of the sun reaching you, touching your body, your mind, making you feel wonderful, and enlivened and enriched within your heart.

Feel your renewed ability to love yourself and to love others, to see clearly and to think with clarity, kindness and purpose. Know that you have no need in your life, in your mind or in your body for anything that places you in unduly stressful situations. Know that you are complete, whole and well, and that your physical, mental, emotional and spiritual selves are as one ...

The Summerland

The light breeze touches you as though in greeting as you enter your garden, and you can feel the peacefulness that exists within this sanctuary surrounding you. The golden rays from the sun touch you lightly, their fingers of warmth bringing joy into your body. The light dapples through the trees and settles around the many flowers, enhancing their beauty. The richly coloured flowers draw the sun's light to them as they stretch themselves ever upwards, seeking the life-enriching rays from the golden globe high in the heavens above.

Your pathway winds in front of you, surrounded by the many trees that stand tall and serene, their branches reaching as though wanting to touch the sky above. There are small bushes clustered on the edges of this pathway, and patches of flowers thrust colour through the greenery as though they feel a need to be noticed. The earth beneath your feet feels soft and warm, and their imprints vanish as you pass, leaving no mark. You feel a lightness of being that you have not experienced for some time.

A small white dove comes to perch on the lower branches of a nearby tree. This bird of peace now takes off, but stops every so often as though it wants you to follow. Follow this dove until you find yourself in a space within your garden that is like none you have entered before. It is as though you have entered another world, one that is filled with golden light, where everything radiates with health and growth, where everything glows with beauty and strength. This is the Summerland, a part of the spiritual realm that is filled with beauty and intensity, of health and wellbeing. The Summerland is also a meeting place for the many departed souls who have since received healing, and whose spirits have been revived until they are now at their optimum in health at all levels.

Peace reigns supreme in the Summerland, this spiritual realm where life is full of beauty. The white dove that led you here has landed on an ornately carved seat that is near a pond. The lilies drift lazily by on the pond, as the light breeze ripples the water. You can hear the croaking of small frogs and the call of the birds as they fly to the branches of the many trees surrounding this place of peace. Look around you and absorb the feelings of warmth and gentleness, of compassion, of love, of being made welcome to this place of beauty.

There are many here in the Summerland who will come forward to be with you, and they come with gentleness and understanding for your grief and your loss. They bring light with them that shines forth, attracting not only animals to them but the smaller and perhaps more gentle creatures that dwell within this sanctuary.

A soul clothed in great radiance is coming forward, surrounded by a pure white light that glows and pulsates with energy. You will recognise this soul as being the one you have loved so deeply, the one you have mourned, the one you feel has left you behind. Open your arms and heart wide, and welcome them and their light to you. Feel the energy pouring through them and coming into your own soul, bringing solace. Feel peace and tranquillity entering your body, your spirit, your mind, soothing your sore heart, bringing a quietening within. You realise that this loved one is at peace and now radiates a harmony that alleviates your grief, allowing you to let go of your grieving and to let the love that exists within your heart to flow fully, without pain.

Speak to your beloved of the many things that have worried you, of the fear you have had for their safety and wellbeing - and see your loved one smile at you. Your beloved has known of these fears and cumbersome worries, and tried to reach you to speak of their love, but the heaviness of your grief has been such that contact has been difficult to make.

Feel your grief lifting, easing your hurt, your pain. Know that life continues in the Summerland, and that the quality of happiness there is such that you would not wish for the return of your loved one.

Put your grieving to one side and see it falling away, like a pile of shavings or dust, into the ground, never to resurface. The need for grieving is past. You have seen your beloved clothed in light and glory, radiating good health and wellbeing. You now know they are happy and contented and that you too can experience these feelings from the memories you will have of this time in your own inner garden, a part of yourself that lives forever.

As you stand in the Summerland, you feel a cloak being placed around your shoulders, bringing with it peace of mind and serenity of spirit. Feel the comfort and warmth this brings to your heart, and feel any remaining sadness that has been with you being lifted and taken away.

Know that there is no death and that the spirit lives on, that the beauty of the soul you have seen and held will always be with you, and that the serenity of your beloved's light and soul will always shine . . .

The Healing Sanctuary

You can hear the birds twittering in welcome as you enter your garden, and their sound reminds you of the peace and serenity that you feel within your sanctuary. Listen and you will also hear the nightingale's beautiful song ringing deep within your garden, resonating with everything that exists there.

There are many animals that have come forward to meet you. Even the fiercest of them is as putty within your special garden, where harmony reigns and all live together in peace. Stroke their fur or feathers as they gather around you, and they will follow you as you go further down your path, going deeper within your garden than you have ever gone before.

Follow the sound of the nightingale's song. You feel as though the magnificence of this bird's music helps in the growth of the plants, the beauty of the flowers that abound around you, and even the warmth of the earth beneath your feet. Allow your feet to take you along your pathway, listening to the nightingale's liquid music and being guided by it, until you come to an exquisite part of your garden that you have not seen before. This beautiful glen is hidden deep within your garden, but you will find that you will have easy access to it whenever you feel the need. The nightingale sits on the lower branch of a huge tree, and you can feel yourself vibrating to the beauty of the sound that comes from the throat of this small bird.

The sun places its healing rays gently around your body, which absorbs their warmth and takes the heat through to the parts of your body that are in need. The blue of the sky is richer and deeper than before, and the gentle breeze moves your hair as though fingers are playing with it. Many trees surround this glen, and the colours and the beauty of the abundant flowers are illuminated as they thrust forward into the light that dapples through the leafy branches.

This glen seems magical. The light is so intense and the healing vibration so strong that you feel the need to lay down upon the velvety grass, its rich green permeating your body as you do so.

Your body starts to feel light and you feel a touch on your shoulders that is so gentle that you are not sure whether you have imagined it. But it is real. The touch has come from one of the many angels who inhabit this healing sanctuary, to which you have been guided. Feel the intensity of the light emanating from this person of wonderful beauty entering your body, enabling the healing to begin. The gentleness and strength of this angel's touch is such that you feel each part of your body resonating to a higher vibration. You can feel your body becoming more centred within, allowing the healing rays to penetrate to areas that have not been reached before.

Look around your beautiful sanctuary and you will see that there are many healing angels, who are now coming forward to assist in your healing. There are some who have come to be observers, while others have brought their wisdom to impart. Hear the sound of their voices raised in song and you will find that this healing sound enters your soul, enters your inner being, working upon you at a deep inner level that resonates to this angelic song. These healing angels are sending their healing thoughts and energy to you, assisting the beautiful person of light who is working on your physical, mental, emotional and spiritual bodies.

Feel your body now floating slightly above the ground, so that the healing energies can flow completely around you, entering your body at all levels. Feel the intensity of the light and energy coming towards you from the angels, and hear their voices raising the healing vibration of their song to yet another level.

Feel the difference within your mind as their healing thoughts and liquid music penetrate deeply within you, and accept the healing that is being given. Feel the joy that comes from having these heavenly bodies working with you, and feel the intensity of their healing rays being absorbed within you. Feel your inner light intensifying until it radiates out from your body, as though to encompass all those in your garden.

This healing sanctuary is always there for you whenever you wish to return. The call of the nightingale will echo through you, bringing the healing vibration to you when you have the need. The beauty of this place and of those who heal there are always accessible for you. Never hesitate to ask for healing from these angels of light . . .

Healing Relationships

You can feel peace and serenity coming around you like a cloak, bringing with it a sense of security within your soul. Your garden is full of light as the golden globe that illuminates your garden of harmony sits high in the heavens above, beaming its rays to where you are. The beautiful tawny lion who sometimes accompanies you in your wanderings is with you, his full mane being ruffled by the light breeze that also moves your hair gently and softly.

You can smell the scent of the many beautifully coloured flowers wafting through the bushes and the trees. The glorious butterflies, in their wonderfully diverse and rich colours, fly from flower to flower in harmony with the bees who are busy gathering their pollen. The roses are in full bloom and their petals glisten with the light dew that has been left from the morning's mist. Small insects make their way along the branches of the many trees that surround you.

The light blue sky has small wisps of clouds passing over it and many birds make their pilgrimage across its expanse, some flying as if towards the sun itself, while others whirl and dive, coming in to land on the branches of the trees that surround you.

The Grandfather Tree is moving his branches as though to welcome you, and his heavy green leaves shine with the sun's light. This old tree has the wisdom of the ages within his bark and crevices, and whenever you have a need for solace or companionship you will always find comfort by resting your back against his thick, solid trunk. Why don't you sit down now and rest against the Grandfather Tree. As you do so you place your hand upon the mane of the magnificent lion who has accompanied you, the lion who shows strength and power, and yet gentleness too.

Like the lion you also have gentleness and strength. Like the tree, you have innate wisdom and knowledge. To heal past relationships or friendships, you can sometimes use the old tree and the lion to show you the best way to accomplish this.

Looking back on past relationships can bring up pain if the relationships ended abruptly, or if there was anger, jealousy, abuse or fear within them. Looking again at a relationship can sometimes not only bring up pain, but other strong emotions that you experienced as a result of the relationship. In order to release these, you need to be like the lion and have the strength within yourself to look at such relationships objectively and with courage. You need also to be wise like the tree, in order to appreciate what you have learned or otherwise gained from the experience.

As you sit with your lion friend and Grandfather Tree, they bring into your mind an understanding of the effects of your relationships, and of the path to healing. They reassure you that from each relationship, even if it ended badly or without resolution, there is much that you have learned that has made you who you are now. You learned what you did *not* want from a relationship, as well as what you want to give to one. Nothing has been lost and much has been gained by your experiences. Yet we can let past relationships have a strongly negative effect on our lives today. You need to look at each relationship, look at each person involved, and release the emotions associated with them, so that you can continue to grow, without being held back by any of the negative feelings that may have been engendered by that particular relationship.

As you are reflecting on your companions' wisdom, you see that the shy nature spirits who inhabit your special garden are placing a screen before you. You realise that upon this screen will unfold those relationships or friendships that have caused you pain. You may find some of these relationships difficult to see again, but sometimes it is necessary to do so in order to heal your emotions and your spirit. Allow your tears to fall, and allow the pain that you have held within you to be released with the tears. See the person with whom you had difficulties, and release them also from the pain and the distress that you both encountered. Allow yourself to view each relationship as an observer, not as the participant, which will help you to not only be objective, but will help to release any pain that remains and assist your healing.

Look within your heart to see what damage was done by the relationship or relationships, and see the darkness within changing. See your heart becoming richer and richer as the memories of failed relationships and the associated pain are released. Forgive the person who caused you the pain, and forgive yourself for the pain you may have caused others.

Look also into the relationships where you might have been the person who initiated the conflict, where you were less than kind, and see yourself being forgiven by the other person.

From each relationship that caused you pain, see hands reaching across to you in friendship. Now see your own hands stretching out before you, towards these hands, in order to heal what has passed. As you do this, have no fear, because these relationships will stay in the past where they belong, and their memories shall be just that - memories - but without the pain that has resided within you for so long.

Feel the freedom within your spirit as you release these memories, and know that any pain that you have had has turned to ashes. You are now strong, without fear. Know that the knowledge and inner wisdom that you carry within will enable you to travel your life's pathway with joy . . .

Healing Your Inner Child

Your garden feels fresh and clean, as though the waters from the heavens have cleansed it, washing everything clean so that it sparkles in the sun's light. The sky is a brilliant blue and the radiance of the sun illuminates the beauty that surrounds you. The gentle breeze sends its light fingers through your hair, and gently moves the petals and leaves of the many flowers and trees that grow within your garden.

Some billowing white clouds are crossing the surface of the rich blue sky, the sun's light turning parts of the clouds golden. The rays from the sun fall around you, its warmth penetrating your body, making you feel as though you are glowing inside. There are many animals coming forward to meet you as always, but this time your beautiful golden lion is also there, to take you deeper into your garden. He emits small growls of pleasure as he pads towards you, placing his mane underneath your hand in order to guide you upon your journey.

As he takes you down your pathway, you see butterflies flying in front of you as though in formation, darting in and out of the many bushes and trees. Some of the butterflies land, not only upon your shoulders, but also upon the mane of your magnificent lion. The smell of the roses drifts towards you, their perfume mingling with that of the other flowers that flourish so well within your special garden. The smell of the magnolia tree mingles with that of the lavender bushes, and the yellow daisies and violets thrust their heads towards the light streaming from the sun, seeking its warmth.

Your gentle lion is taking you into a special part of your garden, where you feel protected and secure, and a sense of peace and serenity surrounds you. Flowers burst forth in profusion and the trees reach high into the heavens, as though wanting to touch the sky itself. Your lion is leading you towards a perfect deep-pink rose whose petals show no signs of bruising. It is as if the rose bush burst forth fully formed from the ground, in a pure unblemished state. There are dew drops glistening on the rose petals, reflecting the light and the warmth of the sun, changing its colour slightly. You become aware that this rose is like you, that it reflects your inner child, the child who is as beautiful as this glorious rose, the child that has always been perfect, and remains so.

See this rose being transformed so that it becomes you, you when you were a small child. See standing before you this beautiful child of creation, this child of the Universe, the one who was and still is you. Tell this child you love her, tell her how special she is, tell her she is perfect and has always been, and that she can do no wrong.

Look and see your special inner child, that small part of yourself that you may not have noticed for some time. Perhaps this beautiful, sensitive child was left behind through not being understood, who suffered hurt or fear, or experienced humiliation or shame, and gather that child into your arms with love.

Let your past come to life before you, and see yourself as this small misunderstood child who asked for love and did not receive it, who asked to be acknowledged and was not, who asked to belong but was not allowed. So that you can go forward as a fully integrated person, with your childhood intact, you need to release the pain from these experiences. Do this now by allowing your tears to come forth, to stream down. Tell this special child of yours that she does not need to be forgiven, as she has done nothing wrong. It is often adults that have caused our inner child to recede, to hide, but other children can also inflict pain. Picture those who have hurt your inner child - whether adults or children - and send forgiveness to them. Perhaps they did not understand your sensitivity, and even if they did and abused you at some level, they still need to be forgiven in order for your beautiful inner child to flourish with health and vitality.

Look at the person who caused you pain and forgive them. Look at the person who abused you and know that it was not your fault, that you were small and insecure, and without knowledge. See if you can find within your heart the ability to release this pain, and to forgive the person who hurt you, so that you can move forward in life.

This small child that you were still exists within you and always will. Love this child with all your heart, with all your mind, with all your soul, and allow her to keep growing, to flourish as a small plant maturing into a beautiful tree, solid and strong, full of wisdom and understanding, going from strength to strength. See your inner child growing, maturing, but still having the wonderment of a small child, being able to see things with a child's clear vision and sensitivity.

Let your beautiful inner child come to full life and know that love not only conquers fear, but is the answer to all aspects of life and living . . .

The Healing Chair

The green of the trees and the grass is very lush, and there are bluebells and roses in pink, mauve and purple. Scattered between these flowers, brilliant yellow daisies and golden daffodils nod their heads in the gentle breeze, while giant yellow sunflowers show their large faces to the sun. The sun is sending its light towards the plants, who feel its warmth penetrating deep into the earth that supports their roots. Its light dapples through the trees, highlighting their green leaves.

The sky is clear, as though it has been wiped clean by a gentle hand so that the sunlight can more easily reach the earth and its plants. As the breeze softly moves your clothes and your hair, you can feel the warmth of the sun's rays caressing your body, going deep within, bringing contentment and peace.

You can hear the musical sounds of birds calling to each other, and the peace and tranquillity within your garden falls around you like a cloak, protectively.

There are some deer approaching who at first appear a little shy, but who gradually become bolder as they come closer to you. They are inquisitive, and nuzzle your hands and face before sometimes darting away, but they always return. Place your hand upon their coats and feel their silkiness beneath your fingers as you pat them. Follow these deer along the pathway and they will take you deeper and deeper into your garden, guiding you until you come to a beautiful lake that glistens with the sun's light. There are white and black swans drifting along its waters, while weeping willows cast their long fingers into the water as though to stir it. Coloured fish dart below the surface of the water, and small green frogs rest on nearby lily pads that easily float upon these serene waters.

Sitting alongside these waters is a large, ornate golden chair, whose arms and back are exquisitely carved. This chair is much larger than you, but, as you sit comfortably upon its expansive seat, you feel as though you belong there. This chair gleams in the sun's light and has retained its warmth. You feel this warmth rising up from the chair, penetrating the pores of your skin as it enters your body, making you feel good inside. This is the chair of healing, which shall always be available for you, by these calm, restorative waters.

This healing chair has been impregnated with healing energies, and these energies gently enter your body before coursing through you, touching each part of your body that is in need. This healing energy is taken deep within you, bringing nourishment and vitality to each of your organs. See it cleansing not only your kidneys, liver and gall bladder, but also enter your spleen, your pancreas and your stomach, removing all toxins from these parts of your body so that your organs can work together in harmony. Feel yourself relaxing within the comfort of this wonderful chair as the healing energy travels through each part of your spine, penetrating and strengthening each bone, each vertebrae, and removing pain or discomfort. The healing you are receiving also cleanses your reproductive system, brings all your organs into alignment within your body, and leaves them enriched and vitalised.

Feel yourself being held by the enormous, beautifully carved arms and back of this magnificent healing chair as you relax upon its seat. You can feel the healing energies going to the place within your body that has the most need, where these energies can do the most good. Allow these energies to enter and to work within your body as you absorb the beauty from your surroundings and the sun's glow from high in the heavens.

Feel a sense of vitality and joy entering your body and feel it connecting within at all levels. Now your heart and mind are working as one, and your body glows with the life and happiness that you have been absorbing. Experience the joy that this healing has brought you, and feel how centred you now are, as all aspects of you have been brought into alignment.

Look around you at nature, at the deer that have come with you, and feel peace and serenity entering your heart, entering the core of your being, making you feel whole and complete, at one with the Universe, at one with all that is . . .

The Moon & Your Emotions

The sky is like black, luxurious velvet, stretching high above you, highlighted by the myriad of stars that sparkle and glow, sending their gentle light down to where you are. Your garden is especially beautiful, bathed in the glow from the stars that hang high in the sky and yet seem close enough to touch.

The earth is soft beneath your feet, and you can hear the rustle of the many leaves on the trees and the bushes as the slight breeze gently moves them. The trees reach high into the heavens, as though they are trying to bring the velvet sky into reach, so that you can touch and feel it. Some of the stars appear to sit upon the trees' uppermost branches, while others appear to form pathways and avenues high in the heavens, to different worlds and universes. The moon hangs full and bright, its magnificent pure light pouring into the garden, surrounding you with its beauty and radiance.

You see in your garden a pond whose surface appears like glass with water lilies floating upon it. You can hear the occasional croaking of the small frogs as they leap from one water lily to the other. Some grass overhangs the sides of the pond, and the light breeze moves the grass as if it were stirring the water with green fingers. Look into the stillness of this pond and you will see the reflection of the glorious moon above, perfect in every way, making you feel that you could touch its light and magnificence.

The nature spirits, the elves and the fairies are coming out to dance under the beauty of this delightful orb, and to show themselves to you, which they seldom do. They are normally reticent to come forward, but tonight they have come to be with you. Listen and you will hear their music, so different to anything you have heard before. You will feel their glorious music entering your emotional body, bringing with it feelings of happiness, joy and peace. These beautiful sprites are beginning to dance and whirl for you, as they have never done before, and their music encourages you to join them. Listen to their violins and feel their music entering your body, enabling you to dance as never before and feel your light clothing floating through the air as you do so.

After you have danced with the small ones, you may like to sit close to the pond that is nearby, in order to absorb the light that is streaming down from the golden moon directly overhead. As you sit comfortably, with the palms of your hands facing upwards, you feel the light from the moon both surrounding your body like a cloak and then pouring down into your body through the top of your head. This powerful light now completely surrounds you, and you can feel its strength and potency as it surges through and enters each part of your body and mind, and fills your heart.

This light enervates you as never before. The power of this light, as it enters your emotional being, gives you the ability to look at your emotions as never before, to understand them as never before, and to alleviate any emotional turmoil you may have experienced. You feel a completeness and a serenity within that you have not felt for some time, and a sense of being connected at all levels of the self envelops you.

Your emotional body, which is a replica of your physical body, stands in front of you in all its wondrous beauty. You can now see how complete this glorious aspect of yourself has become - how aware, how settled, how calm and how knowledgeable it has become from having taken and absorbed the magnificence of the moon's light, from having dealt with and understood the emotions that have needed to be worked through.

Look above you at the luminous moon, with its shadows and its light, which makes you aware of other times and possibilities, and see the light from the stars mingling with that from the moon. Their light streams towards you, touching and illuminating all around you and everything in its pathway.

The Universe stretches above you, making you aware of the endless possibilities of travel and time, of going beyond the dimensions of the earth and of space. The stillness of the night brings a quietude within you, and a feeling of wonder fills your mind, your body, your heart. You become aware that you are connected to the Universe in all its majesty and beauty, your emotions at peace . . .

Your Skeletal Structure

The air is fresh and clean as you enter your garden, and the gentle breeze rustles the leaves on the tall trees, touching your cheek softly and moving through your hair. The sun is beaming down upon you, its warmth touching and penetrating through the pores of your skin, entering your body and making you feel good within. The sky is a rich deep blue, and many small clouds are moving across its surface, sometimes forming faces of people or animals as the breeze changes direction.

The green grass is like a soft carpet under your feet, and the spreading branches of the huge trees are protecting the smaller plants. There are many colourful birds calling to each other as they fly and then come to rest on the lower branches of the leafy trees.

The flowers stretch themselves upwards towards the sun's light, to bask in its glow. The roses, in their many hues, vie in beauty with the tiger lilies and the lilacs, the variety of colours creating a beautiful vision of colour and life. There are many butterflies moving from flower to flower, their colour mingling with that of the bees who are so busy gathering their pollen. The butterflies' fragile wings have very delicate patterns in many colours, and some have a larger wingspan than others. Their wings are glorious - it is as if they have been woven by fairy threads and then dipped into pots of paint that hold all the colours of the rainbow.

In the distance, the mountains stand tall and graceful with power and strength, their peaked caps reaching into the clouds above. The sun's light illuminates these mountains and their pathways, making them accessible to all who feel the need to traverse them. As you begin climbing the pathway of one these mountains, you notice that there are small alpine flowers peeking out from the bushes and the crevices. As you continue on your way, small animals that live on these mountains come to view your progress. You feel comfortable and secure as you go higher, knowing that your feet are being placed firmly and safely upon the pathway that takes you easily and effortlessly ever upwards.

As you climb higher, you find the air easier to breathe than ever before. You now pass through the cloud that has shrouded the top of your mountain from view, and you need only to climb a little further before you are standing on the mountain's very peak. Breathe the air in, taking it deep into your lungs. Feel it strengthening your lungs, taking out the old and stale air and replacing it with fresh, clear mountain air. Bring this clean air deep into the lower part of your lungs, allowing it to circulate and filling them to capacity with its purity.

The sun and its light are closer to you than ever before, and the strength and power of the sun's energy is beaming down towards you. Feel this energy entering your body, going deep within your bones, and take this energy completely through each and every bone of your skeletal structure. Feel these powerful rays penetrating deep inside your bones, adding density to your skeletal structure where it is required. You feel it strengthening your bones until you feel yourself standing straighter and taller than you have been for some time.

And now feel this light penetrating deep within the bones of your skull and your neck, and feel the difference this brings to your cheek bones and jaw. As you feel this light entering the bones at the base of your skull, you find that you can now freely move your head from side to side. The strength of the light is now travelling down and into your spine, and you can feel it entering each and every vertebrae, bringing strength, energy and vitality into each section it touches. Your spine is now as free and as flexible as a young sapling bending in the wind, able to move with ease. Feel the energy and vitality that has entered your skeletal structure coursing through your bones, and see that your bone marrow is also being strengthened, making your bones pliable and giving them new life and stamina.

Take the sun's light into your arms and feel it entering your hands and your fingers. Now take it down into your legs, into your feet and your toes, and feel the strength they now have. You will notice the flexibility you gain within your knee and hip bones as this light penetrates deeply within them, enabling you to move them more freely than has been possible for some time.

Feel the strength you now have within your skeletal structure and how your bones are not only strong, but flexible and free, and able to serve the purposes of your body and mind. Feel the straightness of your spine, with its ability to move with freedom and complete flexibility.

Stretch your arms wide to the Universe, feeling its power and its strength. Know that this power and strength can be, and is, yours . . .

Heavenly Nectar

Your senses are heightened as you enter your special garden, and you are receptive to everything that resides there. Very tiny puffs of clouds are scudding across the beautiful blue sky. The sun hangs like a giant golden ball against the silken sky, sending its light and warmth down to all who care to luxuriate in its glow, warming the earth and its creatures.

The grass beneath your feet feels lovely and soft, yet rich in its texture and colour. The light breeze comes around your body, moving gently through your hair. You can still see the silver drops of moisture on the leaves and grass from the early-morning dew, and the flowers look as though they have been brushed by a gentle wet hand, enhancing their colours.

Stretching their branches, the trees look as if they mean to touch one another, and their uppermost tips reach and welcome the sun's light and warmth that helps their growth. Small bushes grow within the shade of the trees, while others are more exposed, as they need more of the sun's rays. The flowers grow in a colourful profusion, their rich hues complementing the green and yellow of the bushes and trees. Baby's breath threads its way through some of the bushes, while hydrangeas push their bold faces forward, as though seeking attention.

Many birds are coming to land on the lower branches of the surrounding trees, their beautiful plumage making splashes of colour against the dark green leaves. You can hear them calling to each other as they come to land on these branches, while others settle closer to a beautiful fountain that is spurting water from the midst of the pool that you now see before you. The water spurts high into the air, capturing the sun's light before it falls back into the pool, only to be again shot high into the air. You can feel the spray from this fountain settling lightly on your skin, your hair and your clothing, refreshing you with its moisture. A white dove of peace is coming to land near you and, if you listen, you can hear the heavenly music of a flute being played for your ears alone.

Near the fountain is a wide, stone pillar that appears to have weathered eons of time. It is as though it has always been there. An extravagantly large vessel has been placed on this pillar for your use. This urn is made of gold with an intricate pattern etched upon it. It is large and a handle allows you to pour water out of its full, wide lip. With the golden bucket that you find at your feet, fill this magnificent urn with water from the fountain. Now pour this heavenly water over yourself, luxuriating in it as it flows around your body. Its wonderful lightness and freshness washes away any residue of tiredness or lethargy that may be with you.

Drink this heavenly nectar and allow it to go deep within you. Feel it filling you with joy as it touches and penetrates each part of your body, replenishing and renewing your life's vigour, and giving you feelings of joy and happiness. Feel yourself being revitalised by the fountain's water and know that you can always use this magic liquid to be revitalised.

As you now stand over by the pool, you notice that it reflects your image with great clarity. You can see how healthy you have become by drinking so deeply of the heavenly nectar produced by the fountain. As you see your perfect health reflected back to you, your heart is moved to great happiness. Your entire body has been cleansed by using this magic fluid and your energy levels are rising.

You could decide to enter the pool, and stand beneath the falling waters of the fountain itself. Feel them cascade over your head, your shoulders, your entire body, and feel the clarity these waters bring to your mind and the freshness and purity you feel in your body. Luxuriate in these waters and look at the sun's light being reflected within them, magnifying the images of the bushes and trees nearby.

Always come to this sublime fountain when you feel lethargic, or when you feel the need for replenishment and renewal. Know that this heavenly nectar will wash away any toxins or other unwanted matter within your body, as well as any residue of doubt, fear or uncertainty. It will leave you pure and whole . . .

References & Suggested Reading

Byrd, Randolf, 'Positive Therapeutic Effects of Intercessary Prayer in a Coronary Care Unit', *Southern Medical Journal*, July 1988.

Gawler, Grace, *Women of Silence*, Hill of Content, Melbourne, 1984.

Gawler, Ian, *Peace of Mind*, Hill of Content, Melbourne, 1987.

Gawler, Ian, *You Can Conquer Cancer*, Hill of Content, Melbourne, 1984.

Loehr, Reverend Franklin, *The Power of Prayer on Plants*, Doubleday and Co., New York.

Manning, Matthew, *The Link*, Colin Smythe Limited, England, 1973.

Shine, Betty, *Mind to Mind*, Bantam Press, Great Britain, 1989.